LEADERS
Don't Have To Be
SUPER-
HEROES

How to Unmask the Myths and
Claim the *Real* Powers of Leadership

BONNIE L. GALLUP, MA

BGA
PRESS

Fremont, California

Printed in the United States of America
First Printing, 2011

The names and identifying characteristics of the individuals featured throughout this book have been changed to protect their privacy. In some cases, composite characters have been created.

Limits of Liability and Disclaimer of Warranty
The author and publisher shall not be liable for misuse of this material. This book is strictly for informational and educational purposes.

Library of Congress Control Number: 2011910184

ISBN 978-0-9836474-0-9

Published by
BGA Press
491 Lowell Place
Fremont, CA 94536
www.bonniegallup.com

Book Design: Karrie Ross
Editors: Mark Woodworth and Elissa Rabellino

BGA Press books are available at special quantity discounts to use for sales promotions, employee premiums, or educational purposes. Please contact BGA Press at 510-791-8879.

LEADERS
Don't Have To Be
SUPER-
HEROES

Dedication

*I dedicate this book to my parents,
Keith and Nancy—the first leaders in my life.
You are my heroes.*

ACKNOWLEDGEMENTS

*The only people with whom you should try to
get even are those who have helped you.*
—John E. Southard

Whoever said, "You do it yourself but you can't do it alone," must have been referring to writing a book. It's a solitary task to get the words out of your head and on to the page. But I found it takes many creative people to turn those pages into a book—and to keep you going when you can't see the finish line. These special people were my creative support team and I am forever grateful to:

My corporate leaders and clients over the past 20 plus years, for their willingness to become the best leaders they could be. Their stories form the heart of my book and now will inspire other leaders.

Linda Nichole Carrington, my virtual writing partner and colleague, for being dedicated to our writing calls twice a week for two years. Together we went through the ups and downs of writing our first books constantly reminding each other of the wisdom we have to share with the world.

Chris Taylor, an amazing leader and former client, who read every word of my draft manuscript (more than once) and gave me wise and encouraging feedback.

Maureen Simon, dear friend and colleague, for trailblazing the way to publishing a book and sharing with me what she learned along the way.

Chris Nichols, colleague and coach, for helping me see that writing a book was the best next step in my career.

Nancy Shanteau, book coach, for her humor and intuitive way of keeping me writing.

Laren Bright, for his talent in writing the back cover copy and giving shape to this book.

Mark Woodworth and Elissa Rabellino, for editing in ways that inspired me to rewrite, rewrite, rewrite and rewrite.

Karrie Ross for her extraordinary talent in designing the book cover and interior layout.

Susan Bercu and **Larry Smith** for sharing their experiences in book publishing so that I could avoid some of the bumps in the road that they discovered.

Megan Gallup, for being the most amazing daughter, my biggest fan, and giving me the viewpoint of the millennial generation.

Joe Gallup, my husband of 31 years, for listening to endless rewrites, doing creative cover design ideas, logo designs and supporting me unconditionally through everything it takes to run my consulting business and write a book.

My mother, Nancy, for her gift of pure Scottish courage and for *always* having my back.

TABLE OF CONTENTS

Part III: Put It All Together

BEFORE YOU BEGIN: SOME THINGS YOU NEED TO KNOW

*The truth is many people aspire to be leaders
but few will prepare. Those who become effective
leaders are the ones who prepare to lead.*
—T. R. Warren

Why I Wrote This Book

It was a crisp, fall day in New York City. I'd flown in from California to work with a leader who headed up a large, global division of a worldwide consulting company. This company was full of brilliant, accomplished people and the person I would be coaching was one of their brightest. I was called in because he was struggling in his leadership role.

When I met him he looked overwhelmed and exhausted. I began to understand why when he described the stress he was under and the lack of support he got from his team. As I asked more questions it became clear that he saw his leadership role as a solo act: he was the one who took responsibility for everything that went on with his six person, senior leadership team. He actually used the metaphor that, as the leader, he felt like he was pulling an entire airplane that couldn't seem to take off by itself. When I asked where his team was in his imaginary metaphor, he paused and said, "They aren't onboard and they aren't helping me pull. In fact, they aren't there at all."

Curious, I asked him to describe himself as a leader using as many adjectives as he could. He used only one: "Reluctant." Then I asked him to give me some adjectives for how he would describe a successful leader—someone he admired. He gave me about ten adjectives that sounded like a composite of Gandhi, Steve Jobs, Donald Trump, Warren Buffet, Bill Gates—and Superman. To him, successful leaders were those who had appeared on the cover of Time magazine, were quoted in the Wall Street Journal and perhaps had even won the Nobel Peace Prize. He summarized by saying, half-kiddingly, "A great leader, is everything I am not."

From A Coach's Perspective

This man was in pain and I was the first person he could trust to just listen to his frustration. He was actually doing a great job in terms of work results. Revenue streams for his group were among the highest in the company. He was, however, operating with some heavy-duty expectations for who he was "supposed" to be as a leader. And he was tired, very tired, of driving himself and not feeling like he was living up to his own high standards. And where exactly was his team?

After carefully considering what he had communicated, I looked at him and said, "Of course you are not all that—and neither are they. You've just described a superhero, not a real person." A look of relief flashed across his face. For the first time since we had met, I could see him visibly relax.

Dismantling a Myth

This high performer had a bad case of the "leader as superhero syndrome" and it was inhibiting him from recognizing the kind of leader he actually was and becoming the best leader he could be. His unexamined, lofty ideal of what a leader *should* be was killing him.

We worked together for the next six months to dismantle his superhero myth and build a realistic model for his leadership—clarifying what kind of leader he aspired to be and what he needed to do to engage his team. We gave him more comfortable "clothes" to wear—not the cape, mask and spandex of his "ideal leader," but ones more suited to who he actually was—a dedicated, intelligent, hard working leader with a team that needed guidance in stepping up to the plate. If he was ever going to stop pulling that metaphoric airplane all by himself, he would need their help getting it onto the tarmac and airborne.

This experience started me thinking about how many other leaders suffer under their own well intended but unrealistic expectations for their leadership performance. I realized that with most of the leaders I coached there was some underlying "myth" about leaders needing to be superheroes—or some other lofty image or even some not so lofty image—that was getting in the way. Surfacing those myths was an important part of their leadership development.

The Bottom Line

I wrote this book to assure you that leadership is less about the heroics and more about how you authentically lead and inspire people—every day. I want to show you how to unmask your own self-limiting beliefs and to share with you the stories of real leaders who were willing to take an honest look at themselves and become the best leaders they could be. I hope that their stories and what they learned will become a pathway for moving your own leadership in a new and better direction.

Who Can Benefit from This Book?

When I asked a trusted senior leader whom she thought would benefit most from reading *Leaders Don't Have to Be Superheroes,* she replied without hesitating, "I'd give copies of the book to all my leaders with yellow post-it notes on the pages I thought they should pay attention to."

I liked her response, since I envision this book being used by leaders at all levels, in any organization, who want to both learn and practice the subtle yet powerful qualities of effective leadership. In fact, I liked her response so much that I recommend you get some yellow post-it notes and do the same.

What My Experience Has Revealed

After more than two decades of coaching and training leaders, I began to see certain trends, in addition to the superhero myth, emerge from the leaders who came to me for coaching. These trends reflected issues that, if not addressed, seemed to stop the positive momentum of their careers—not to mention, be the cause of breakdowns in getting desired results.

These trends I observed, which I call Leader-*slips,* were distilled from my coaching work with leaders who were already successful and wanted to be even more effective in their leadership roles. These were not leaders who were failing—they just weren't paying enough attention to some very critical areas of their leadership.

Leader-*slip* Trends I Observed

The leaders were not:

- Aware of their true leadership impact
- Seeking feedback regarding their impact
- Clear on how subtle leadership can actually be
- Integrating specific leadership actions as a part of their daily routines
- Tending to the relationships required to maintain and sustain long-term success
- Systematically paying attention to all the areas of their leadership territory
- Constantly learning and evolving as a leader
- Inspiring themselves so that they could better inspire others

You will see these Leader-*slip* trends underlying the problems each leader faces in the stories explored throughout *Leaders Don't Have to Be Superheroes.*

Note that these Leader-*slip* trends pertain to *leadership* effectiveness and not the technical expertise of the leaders. Each trend points to a critical aspect of good leadership that isn't necessarily taught in business or technical schools—these are the "differences that make the difference" between a poor, average or excellent leader. My research is based on my experience with my clients, however, what I observed has been confirmed in books and other research literature that I have read in building my consulting expertise.

The Real Heroes of This Book

Leaders Don't Have to Be Superheroes tells the stories of successful leaders who were courageous enough to admit they could be better leaders and were willing to learn how. These leaders also worked in organizations that recognized the value of good leadership to their bottom line and backed that up with time and resources to help their leaders develop.

I am inspired by each and every one of the men and women I have written about. I feel privileged to have supported, guided, and walked beside them. Our work together was based on a mutual trust and respect. Although I have not used their real names, I hope that, if they recognize themselves in the stories I share, they will feel honored.

May their courage inspire you to be the best leader *you* can be.

HOW TO GET THE MOST
FROM THIS BOOK

To match the pace of the intelligent and busy leader's life, this book is designed to be:

- A quick read
- Based on challenges real leaders face every day
- Full of questions to stimulate thinking
- A call to action

Plan to Participate

Do you ever wonder if other leaders deal with the same issues you do, and how they handle them? As you read the stories in *Leaders Don't Have to Be Superheroes*, you'll be right there in the trenches with successful leaders as they address challenging issues and learn subtle, yet important, new ways of thinking and behaving. Take notes and apply what you learn from them to your own leadership situations. This book is a call to action with tools to help you.

Part I:
Unmask the Myths

Part I presents vital contextual information about leadership that sets the stage for what's to come. As you explore some of your basic beliefs about being a leader, ask yourself whether you need to challenge, update, or radically change those beliefs to move your leadership to the next level. This section includes questions to get you thinking.

Part II:
Claim the *Real* Powers of Leadership

In Part II, there are 15 *Real* Powers of Leadership that emerge from the stories in each chapter. You'll see how each leader uses these *Real* Powers to turn their problematic situations around. You can read the chapters in order or read the ones that interest you first. Just becoming aware of the issues presented in this section can open the door to new thinking about your own leadership practices and the impact you have on those you lead. There are questions and challenges to get you engaged and ready to test out the *Real* Powers for yourself.

Part III:
Put It All Together

Part III offers some important tools to guide you in integrating and immediately applying what you explored in Part II. A summary table of the 15 *Real* Powers of Leadership will help you to identify which of the *Real* Powers you may want to develop further.

Another Way to Get the Most from This Book

Many leaders I coach use team learning to keep their direct reports aware of the importance of continually developing their leadership awareness and skills. These leaders select a book each quarter to read and discuss during staff meetings. It's an excellent strategy for keeping leadership development as an ongoing, relevant topic in your organization.

As you read *Leaders Don't Have to Be Superheroes* consider how it applies to you—then think about how you might use this book for learning and discussion with your team.

Begin with an Open Mind

To increase the value you get from reading *Leaders Don't Have to Be Superheroes*—begin with an open mind.

When any real progress is made,
we unlearn and learn anew what we thought
we knew before.

—Henry David Thoreau

Part I

Unmask the Myths

It is impossible for a man to learn what he
thinks he already knows.
—Epictetus

We keep moving forward, opening new doors,
and doing new things, because we're curious and
curiosity keeps leading us down new paths.
—Walt Disney

Part I presents vital contextual information about leadership that sets the stage for what's to come. As you explore some of your basic beliefs about being a leader, ask yourself whether you need to challenge, update, or radically change those beliefs in order to move your leadership to the next level.

CHAPTER 1

DEBUNK THE MYTH OF LEADER AS SUPERHERO

*No matter how many times you save the world, it always
manages to get back in jeopardy again. Sometimes
I just want it to stay saved! You know, for a little bit?
I feel like the maid; I just cleaned up this mess! Can we
keep it clean for...for ten minutes?"*
—Mr. Incredible, in the movie *The Incredibles*

*When leaders take back power, when they act as
heroes and saviors, they end up exhausted, overwhelmed,
and deeply stressed.*
—Margaret J. Wheatley

Removing the Cape, Mask, and Spandex

The myth of leader as superhero puts a lot of pressure on leaders.
The myth runs deep, especially in American culture. As a leader
working hard to do your best, you may not even be aware of how
it lurks in the background as a set of expectations you may never
quite live up to.

I often ask leaders I coach to describe their idea of an excellent
leader. Their descriptions often include attributes like these: "wise,"

"revered," "works tirelessly to achieve goals," "charismatic," "vision-ary," "unflappable," "knows what to do and when to do it." Together, we review their descriptions and decide that the only thing missing is "leaps tall buildings in a single bound" and "walks on water." After a good laugh, we conclude that having unrealistic expectations about leadership can often be more defeating than inspiring.

Think about your own expectations of leaders. Do you expect them to demonstrate qualities and talents above and beyond what is humanly possible for one person to possess? Do you expect that of yourself? We've been gravely disappointed by recent news reports of larger-than-life athletes, politicians, and captains of industry who lost their balance and fell from their lofty pedestals. Perhaps they fell farther and harder from those pedestals because in our desire to create superheroes, we granted them superpowers and qualities they never possessed.

Real Leaders, Real Power

Leaders are human, not superheroes. Leadership is most often unheroic, unshowy, and unassuming. Yet it takes a lot of character and courage, day in and day out, to be a good leader. In real life, leadership is more like a series of decisions and actions that direct and inspire others—every day. Although it has its share of big, spotlight moments, leadership is also subtler than you might imagine.

Think about the last time your boss merely raised an eyebrow when you proposed a breakthrough idea of yours. That one quizzical look can transmit powerful messages that signal the leader's thinking about how much risk is acceptable, how open that leader is to new ideas, and how much that leader may (or may not) trust you.

Real leadership lies in the subtleties of those moments. I wonder if your boss knew how one look could potentially stop innovation in your department dead in its tracks. The least it could do was have you think twice about presenting your next out-of-the-box idea. That seemingly ordinary moment was packed with meaning, without a word being spoken by the leader. Leadership can be that subtle.

Another thing about superheroes is that they appear only when grave danger is looming. They act alone, save the day, and then retreat into their secret identity until the next crisis. You may know of leaders who seem to use this as their leadership model. However, *real* leaders who use their *real* powers handle it much differently.

A recent research study from the © Center for Creative Leadership (CCL) says it well:

> It's no longer the time of the heroic leader—the leader who walks in and takes up all the space in the room. The job of today's leader is to create space for other people—a space in which people can generate new and different ideas; a space where seemingly disparate departments and people in the organization come together and have meaningful conversation; a space in which people can be more effective, more agile, and more prepared to respond to complex changes.
> —Andre Martin, CCL white paper, *The Changing Nature of Leadership*, p.19

The true powers of leaders today, more than ever before, have to do with building relationships, gaining trust, influencing, communicating, collaborating, inspiring, and setting an example. And what's interesting is that these are the same issues that leaders brought to our coaching sessions as challenges they faced in achieving their goals.

The truth is you don't have to be a superhero to be a super leader. (Is that a sigh of relief I hear?) But you may have to change your beliefs about what leadership is and what will make you an excellent leader.

> *We are what we repeatedly do. Excellence,*
> *then, is not an act, but a habit.*
> —Aristotle

Pause and Reflect

Is there a superhero myth lurking in the background of your own thoughts about leadership? Are you willing to explore any other unexamined beliefs you may have in order to become a better leader?

CHAPTER 2

UPGRADE YOUR OPERATING SYSTEM

*In times of change, learners inherit the Earth,
while the learned find themselves beautifully equipped
to deal with a world that no longer exists.*
—Eric Hoffer

Shift Happens: New Mind-Sets Required

Think about how the world has changed since you began your working life. It's clear that nothing today is "business as usual," nor should we harbor hopes that what was "usual" will return. *Evolve or perish* is today's reality. Can leadership stay the same when everything around it has shifted so dramatically?

In the midst of chaos lies opportunity. And to take advantage of that opportunity, it is essential that we avoid dragging outdated thinking and beliefs into the new territory and using them to design our future. We also have choices about the quality of that future. An important question to be asking now is: What kind of leadership is needed for today's global business challenges?

Your role as leader needs to keep evolving. But what's required is more than just *doing* things differently. Leaders need to think differently and perceive differently. All real paradigm shifts start with the way we think, what we believe, and our underlying assumptions.

Are You Due for an Upgrade?

When technology becomes outdated, we upgrade the software and operating systems. Now may be a good time to check the mental software and systems you are running about leadership. If you don't upgrade, you'll be caught in the same old struggles as before.

The research white paper from the © Center for Creative Leadership, *The Changing Nature of Leadership* by Andre Martin, quoted in Chapter 1, also states that "the definition of effective leadership has changed in the last five years." It goes on to describe *how* it has changed: "Leaders face challenges that go beyond their individual capabilities....Interdependent work is the foundation of effective leadership. ...The new leader needs to achieve bottom-line results, but must do this through collaboration, teamwork, and innovation."

The paper goes on to say, "Today's leaders need right-brain skills—empathy, inventiveness, and quest for meaning—to achieve professional success and personal satisfaction. In fact, the best MBA programs are moving in this direction and offering soft-skill training, such as how to build stronger teams and how to communicate more effectively."

The way work gets done is changing. Those "pesky people issues," which my coaching clients wished would go away, are fast becoming where they need to focus.

The style of a successful leader is changing. Jim Collins, in the research for his book *Good to Great: Why Some Companies Make the*

Leap . . . and Others Don't, discovered a leadership style that took companies from *good to truly great.* He calls it Level 5 Leadership, the highest level in a hierarchy of executive capabilities. He describes a Level 5 Leader as "a study in duality: modest and willful, shy and fearless." He found that the leader with the larger-than-life persona was *not* the person at the helm of companies that were moving from good to great.

What appears to be emerging is a new focus for leadership and a new kind of leader. Not that they haven't been there all along. It's just that these characteristics are what need to be called forward in these new and challenging times.

Change Begins with How You Think

The most important factor in transforming leadership today is confronting every leader's willingness to *unlearn* what he or she knows and to change.

So what could stop *you* from transforming your own ideas about who you are as a leader and, if needed, making some changes? Take a look at some common ways of thinking that might discourage you from trying:

Resistance to breaking the mold. "What leaders did for me is good enough for my employees. Why should *I* change when I don't see other leaders doing things differently?"

No new model. "I can't be a different kind of leader until I know exactly what to do."

Feeling overwhelmed. "There's so much to do; where do I start?"

Impatience. "OK, I'll try something new, but I want to see results *now*."

Possible negative perceptions. "How can I change and still be credible? People will think I didn't know what I was doing."

If any of these sound familiar, you might want to look at whether your leadership mind-set is going to propel you into the next decade, or even into the next year. Change is never comfortable, but trying to stay the same when everything around you is changing may not be the best strategy. At the least, be open to exploring new ways of seeing and thinking about your current leadership challenges.

Challenge Your Own Leadership Status Quo

If you are currently doing well as a leader, why would you want to change anything? As in business and sales, so it follows in leadership: "You can't just keep doing what you did and expect to get what you got." You may want to stick with what works for you, but you might eventually wonder why you aren't being as effective as you used to be.

In my coaching practice, I encourage my clients to explore new ways of looking at their distinctive style of leadership. For some, it's the first time they've even considered *how* they lead as separate and distinct from the goals they pursue. With support, they have risked challenging their own leadership status quo and made some necessary changes. Some have gone from reserved, somewhat reticent leaders to leaders who step up and claim their role; they are now clear on how they create value. Others have changed from action-based leaders with their hands in every project to leaders who focus instead on building an environment where their employees can succeed.

Did they make mistakes along the way? Sure. Did they feel uncomfortable at first? You bet they did. But all of them have improved their leadership effectiveness and are glad they went through the challenging learning curve.

Why? Because there is less friction within their organizations and with other departments with whom their teams interact. Their leadership role and their impact have become clear and more positive. Defining their own compelling goals for success has ignited their personal commitment. They know that if they aren't growing and learning, they can't expect it of those they lead.

The First Step

Think about your current leadership experience and then answer the following questions:

- Could you be unknowingly caught in an outdated, unexamined model of leadership? How would you know?
- When is the last time you made a deliberate, positive change in the way you lead or in who you are as a leader?
- Have you defined who you *want* to be as a leader? Are you taking steps each day to become that leader?

You can't do the same things you are doing and simply *expect* different results. You also don't have to assume that you will change everything you are currently doing. Start changing things in increments. Test for what works. Keep what does, and then phase out the rest. Work with it. You may need to adjust or change only 10 percent of what you are currently doing. Knowing what that 10 percent is will be essential.

Be willing to take an honest look at how you think about and deliver on your leadership promise. Be sure you have defined that promise and stay open to learning new ways of leading.

Pause and Reflect

The times are changing—is your leadership changing with the times?

CHAPTER 3

OWN YOUR FORCE FIELD

While we are free to choose our actions,
we are not free to choose the consequences of our actions.
—Stephen R. Covey

Take a Good Look in the Mirror

What you have experienced under the leadership of others is the same influence you have over those you lead. I call it the Leadership Force Field. To illustrate the idea of a leader's Force Field, think about the best and worst leaders for whom you have worked. What were the qualities of the best leaders, in contrast to the worst? What kind of environment did each create through his or her beliefs, words, and behaviors? In which environment did you want to do your best, and why?

The Leadership Force Field is what you were experiencing. It has everything to do with the leader's character and the way he or she leads. Organizations become the reflections of their leaders. That's why it is so important for you to know who you are and be aware of your leadership impact. You want to be sure that your mind-set, and what you say and do, are what you want to see reflected.

Being in the spotlight highlights and exposes nuances of your beliefs, thinking, and behavior that you may not even be aware of. But those you lead don't miss a thing, as they align themselves to be in step with you—or not. Soon your entire team or organization will have a culture based on the mind-set, mood, and tone set by you as the leader.

Why is this important? If the tone you set fails to both motivate and encourage productivity, innovation, and creativity from the people you lead, then you will see a reduction in the quality and quantity of results achieved. You may also have difficulty attracting and holding on to top talent.

How a Leadership Force Field Works

The Leadership Force Field actually works in quite subtle ways. Here is an example: A new CEO came on board one of my client companies, and I noticed that he wore pinstriped, long-sleeved shirts every day. In the course of a few months (a few weeks for early adopters), I watched an entire executive team who usually wore polo shirts start showing up in pinstriped shirts, until everyone around the table was dressed just like the CEO (and, yes, that included some women). When I mentioned my observation to several executive team members, they had no idea what I was talking about. Hadn't they always worn pinstriped shirts? The Leadership Force Field is *that* subtle, and influences much more than clothing choices.

As a leader, *you* are the message—the instrument through which you lead. Your character, your integrity, the way you walk your talk—all speak louder than any message you may try to send. Knowing what messages you are sending ensures that you are sending the right ones.

Here are ways to begin understanding the qualities of your own Leadership Force Field:

- It's difficult to know the impact of your own Leadership Force Field unless you take it seriously and check it out. Be curious. Observe how people react to you. Self-observation and awareness are important first steps.
- We can't always see ourselves as others see us. Feedback is a gift—so ask for it and *accept* it, formally and informally and on a consistent basis, from trusted colleagues, bosses and employees.
- Hire a leadership coach to help you understand how you come across. A coach can do the following:
    - o Interview others to collect information on the impact you are having
    - o Observe you in action and give you unbiased feedback
    - o Clarify the feedback so that you know what to do differently
    - o Support and guide you in making any necessary changes

The Origin of Your Leadership Force Field

Here's what is important to know about your Leadership Force Field: it comes with the territory, whether you acknowledge it or not. And you are responsible for it, yet you can't manipulate it— the truth always comes out sooner or later.

Two quotes that get to the heart of the matter:

> "Good leadership starts from the inside of an individual leader, then it is demonstrated outwardly. Good leadership is founded in a state of being, not just doing. It is about your outlook, your orientation, your character, and your inner thoughts and emotions." —Ken Blanchard

"Becoming a leader is synonymous with becoming your-self. It's that simple, and that difficult." —Warren Bennis

And to borrow another saying, good leaders declare "the buck *stops* with them." It can also be said of good leaders that the true spirit of the organization *starts* with them.

Questions to Consider

- Would you say that your Leadership Force Field inspires others, creating an environment in which people want to (and can) do their best work? How would you know?
- Do you have systems in place for getting high-quality, regular feedback on your leadership impact?

Pause and Reflect

What is the impact of your Leadership Force Field? Have you checked lately?

CHAPTER 4

STEP UP AND CLAIM IT

*Leadership is a scary thing. That's why few people want
to step up to the plate. There are many people who
want to be matadors, only to find themselves in the ring
with 2,000 pounds of bull bearing down on them,
and then discover that what they really wanted was
to wear tight pants and hear the crowd roar.*
—Steve Farber

Who's "They"?

I recently facilitated a meeting for a group of 60 directors in a high-tech company. They were having animated discussions about how to achieve their upcoming revenue goals. When we discussed what could get in the way of implementing their plans, they were all clear in stating that it was up to the leadership of the company to make some important decisions and implement some important changes. They felt that until *they* (the leadership) did, there was nothing much *they* (the directors) could do.

Puzzled by their remarks, I checked my roster to make sure these were the directors of the company and not another individual contributor group that I was scheduled to talk with that week. After confirming that, in fact, each was a director of a key area within the company, I asked: "If you aren't the leaders of the company, who is?" Their silence in response to my question gave us all reason to pause—why didn't they consider themselves part of the "they" that was leading the company?

Step In, Step Up

As a leader, you step into leadership territory every day. Those you lead make a space for you to lead them. It's your job to claim the role and get good at it.

If you don't realize what you need to pay attention to, then your team/group/organization operates like a plane without a pilot or a ship without a captain—not very effectively. Sometimes people in organizations with leaders who abdicate the territory can be heroic and accomplish much, in spite of the lack of leadership. You have to wonder how much more they could accomplish with a leader who has stepped up to the plate.

The main flow of work within companies consists of interactions among people. If you aren't tending to those human interactions, greasing the wheels with clear direction, fine-tuning it with feedback, and providing encouragement and inspiration—all of these on a regular basis—then you are neglecting a large part of your leadership territory.

Too often, leaders fail to spend sufficient energy engaging their most powerful resources: their people. They are in a leadership role usually for doing what they do best and are rewarded for: getting results, often regardless of the impact on people.

The challenge for leaders is defining and crafting their own leadership style as they achieve those bottom-line results. They are no longer individual contributors with projects and deliverables that define their work, yet that is the experience they bring to the job.

I'm not just talking about new leaders here. Leaders at the vice-president and director levels have asked me: "How can I still be of value when I support other people achieving the wins? What is my value now? Who can see what I'm doing? I miss the excitement of being directly engaged in the action."

These leaders are in pure leadership territory, which lacks the familiar landmarks, challenges, and risks that they have been used to all during their careers. Leaders must establish new metrics for their success, since that success has less and less to do with their individual achievements. If they use old metrics (this is more common than you might think), they aren't giving themselves an accurate way to measure how they are creating value as a leader. It's easier for them to recognize their success in terms of leadership when they use the correct indicators.

You'll learn a variety of metrics for leadership as you explore the 15 *Real* Powers of Leadership in Parts II and III.

Questions to Consider

- Do you see your leadership role as consisting of a distinct set of knowledge, skills, and behaviors that you need to constantly be aware of applying? And ones that you need to continue improving?
- Look at your activities each and every quarter. How much time do you spend steering the ship—keeping your human resources on course, focused, alert, and inspired to reach their goals? Be honest. I coach many leaders who are working on their own special projects and agendas which makes their attention to their entire group sporadic at best. They also may give more attention to the areas they know and understand, rather than to those they don't understand or have a specific interest in. Often they step in only when something goes wrong.

- Have you ever mapped out your entire leadership territory? That is, have you made a visual representation showing *all* the areas that need your attention in order for your organization to achieve success and remain successful?
- Have you reset your personal metrics for success as a *leader*?

The most important thing you can do, when in a leadership role, is to step up and claim it. The second most important thing is to get good at it, just as you would when pursuing any other endeavor in which you wanted to develop a level of excellence. The third thing is to measure your leadership effectiveness with the appropriate metrics so that you know how you create value—and when you are successful. Take some time to update your internal success metrics. Success as a leader feels different than when you personally carried the ball across the finish line.

Pause and Reflect

Have you stepped up and claimed your leadership role and territory? Are you committed to getting good at leading and inspiring others? How do you measure your own success as a leader?

Pause and Reflect

I cannot teach anybody anything;
I can only make them think.
— Socrates

Before moving on to Part II, take time to pause and reflect once again on the questions posed in Part I. If these questions get you thinking about *your* leadership and spark your curiosity for "opening new doors and doing new things," it's worth taking another look.

Debunk the Myth of Leader as Superhero

- Is there a superhero myth lurking in the background of your own thoughts about leadership?
- Are you willing to explore any other unexamined beliefs you may have in order to become a better leader?

Upgrade Your Operating System

- The times are changing—is your leadership changing with the times? Or could you be unknowingly caught in an outdated, unexamined model of leadership? How would you know?

- When was the last time you made a deliberate, positive change in the way you lead or in who you are as a leader? Is your leadership changing and evolving?

Own Your Force Field

- Would you say that your Leadership Force Field inspires others, creating an environment in which people want to (and can) do their best work? How would you know?
- Do you have systems in place for getting high-quality, regular feedback on your leadership impact?

Step Up and Claim Your Territory

- Have you stepped up and claimed your leadership *role* and *territory*? Are you committed to getting good at it? How do you measure your success as a leader?

Bonus Question

- What other questions could you be asking yourself to ensure that you are the best leader you can be?

Part II

Claim the *Real* Powers of Leadership

With great power comes great responsibility.
—Ben Parker, *Spider Man 2*

Part II introduces you to the unshowy, unheroic, 15 *Real* Powers of Leadership. You'll read the stories of real leaders and how they used these powers to turn their situations around.

You may not see yourself in every story but you may think other stories were written about you. Pay attention to the "How You Know When..." section of each chapter, it may help you to see how a particular issue might be showing up for you in a way you can recognize.

The stories are constructed like a coaching experience so you can see how through feedback, inquiry and action the leaders resolved the problems they faced. See what you can learn from each of the stories presented. In the Summary section of Part II, you'll explore what each of these leader's stories have in common.

CHAPTER 5

THE BLAME GAME: PLAY IT AND NOBODY WINS

The search for someone to blame is always successful.
—Robert Half

It is human nature to search for the guilty party when things go wrong. Somehow it feels better, knowing who did it and that no one thinks it's you. Not to mention that being *right* gives the ego a huge boost. But by the time the finger pointing is over, everyone involved is so defensive and running for cover that the openness required for problem solving is often destroyed. Playing *The Blame Game* is expensive. It erodes relationships, inhibits trust, and impedes workflow.

Real Power #1: Create a Safe, Collaborative Environment

Phil's Story: Playing to Win

Phil is a vice president in a high-tech company who frequently complained that certain other departments were throwing up road-blocks so that his people couldn't get what they needed to do their jobs. He was consistently annoyed that *their* systems were screwed up and thought if *they* would get their acts together things would go more smoothly for him and his organization. Phil openly blamed the other departments any time his team encountered problems working with them.

As a result, Phil's staff took up the blaming stance and tensions increased at all levels. Worse yet, things weren't changing, and his organization seemed to be deadlocked with several other groups. Not a good scenario, since their departments all relied heavily on each other.

In one of our coaching sessions, I asked Phil: "If you *think* blame, your behavior and words will convey that message. Is that what you want other people to experience—that they are being blamed for the current problems?" He replied that he had never really thought about it. They were wrong, and once they owned up to it, he could then tell them what they needed to do instead. In fact, he actually was trying to tell them what to do differently now, but they just weren't listening.

I then asked him how taking that position was working. Was any-thing changing for the better? Were the other departments admitting their guilt and asking what they could do differently? He asked if I thought he should take the blame for something they were doing. I asked him why anyone had to take the blame—wasn't the real goal a better working relationship so that problems, which were inevitable, could be solved? He had to think about that, since *The Blame Game* was about being right and winning, not about building relationships and collectively solving problems.

When in Doubt, Check It Out

To give Phil a reality check, I interviewed the four senior leaders involved, to hear their side of the deadlock. They each said that if Phil would just come to the table admitting that his team might also be contributing to the problem, they would be willing to work with him. Right now, all they could do was defend themselves. They were not going to work toward any solution if it meant having to admit that their groups were solely the cause of the problems. They thought Phil had backed them into a corner, and they didn't like it one bit. It was also not surprising to learn that they blamed Phil's department for most of the problems.

After hearing the feedback from the other leaders, Phil reluctantly admitted that they most likely would not come to their senses and give him the win he needed. His current tack would just get him more of the same: resistance.

So Phil agreed to try something different. We role-played how he would go to each leader and say (and mean it) that his team was willing to do whatever it could to help things work better between their departments. He would ask the leaders how they saw the problem and what they thought his group could do differently. He would listen to their responses and take notes. He would offer to set up problem-solving teams consisting of people from his group and theirs, to find out specifically how they could work better together. He would ask if they would be open to making changes in their areas too, if that's what these problem-solving teams identified.

Phil had a meeting with each leader and followed the plan we had rehearsed. The other leaders were surprised by his new approach but felt he was sincere. They agreed to share their perspectives and support any needed changes their teams might need to make.

Phil Changes the Game

Phil observed how easily the deadlock of *The Blame Game* was broken when he made the first positive move. He also saw how work and progress slowed while he waited for the other groups to admit their guilt. Although he had to give up the ego rush of being right, he saw how owning the problem and working toward the solution together created a better outcome for everyone. He had to admit that the *real* game is getting problems solved and people working together smoothly.

As Phil began to model this new approach with his team members and coach them on how to have more neutral and fact-based discussions with the other departments, his entire organization benefited from the newly formed lines of communication. The groups went on to develop new systems that assisted all of the departments in interfacing more effectively. Those systems positioned the departments to avoid problems and set them up to work through any conflicts that did occur.

Phil began to value the fact that things were running more smoothly. He could see how shifting his thinking had changed his own behavior and that the influence it had on his team was profound.

COACHING RECOMMENDATIONS

If you see *The Blame Game* being played in your organization, check whether you might inadvertently be setting it up or supporting it as the rules of play.

The real challenge with *The Blame Game* is that it is so pervasive, it has almost become the norm for the way organizations work and the way people treat each other to get the work done. Here's where it's important to step out of the status quo and ask yourself: "What's a better way to create the problem-solving environment and alliances we need to be even more successful in the long run?" Think carefully about what would need to be changed in your organization for problems to get solved without blame having to be assigned.

Play a New Game

So what's the antidote for *The Blame Game*? It's simple: play a different game. It's called *The Take Responsibility and Be Accountable Game*. The rules for this game are as follows:

- Everyone owns a piece of the problem and a part of the solution. Blaming gets you in the penalty box.
- To win, you must build relationships within teams and across teams.
- Admitting mistakes gets you extra points. (Phil could also have said that he had been wrong in his original approach and asked the others if they would give him another opportunity to come at the problems in a different way.)
- Communication needs to be honest and forthright, even if that feels uncomfortable. *The Blame Game* buries information as people try to protect themselves. *The Take Responsibility and Be Accountable Game*, by contrast, asks everyone to contribute what he or she knows, so that the solution can be based on accurate, complete data. There needs to be a feeling of safety for people to speak up if the information may be controversial.

When, as a leader, you start thinking from the perspective of *The Take Responsibility and Be Accountable Game*, your actions and behavior will shift. Instead of the hunt for whom to blame, your questioning strategy might sound something like this: "What is the problem we need to solve? What were the contributing factors? Who is involved or affected by this? How can we get accurate information from all parties? How do we work together to find the cause and solve the problem?"

A big difference between the two games is the starting point: *The Take Responsibility and Be Accountable Game* begins in neutral territory. When things are neutral, people can be more honest and open with information, and the energy shifts from guarded and withholding to exploring what's really going on and how to fix it.

The bottom line: Looking for root *cause* is not the same as looking for root *blame*. As the leader, you name the game that others will play. It will also be the game that *you* are playing. Be sure you know which game you are modeling, for you'll be setting it up as "the way we do things around here."

HOW YOU KNOW WHEN YOU'RE PLAYING
The Blame Game

- You tend to get locked into your position and have a strong need to be right.
- You see things as *us* versus *them*, even within your own company.
- Your belief is that assigning blame is part of the problem-solving process.
- Others may also be resisting or blaming you. When it comes to blame, if you give it out, you usually get it back from others.

How to Recognize Which Game is Being Played

In *The Blame Game* people will:	In *The Responsibility & Accountability Game* people will:
• Immediately ask, "*Who* is responsible for this problem?"	• Immediately ask, "*What* went wrong?" and gather the facts.
• Seek one person to focus on as the sole source of the problem.	• Acknowledge that multiple causes are most likely involved.
• Avoid sharing information to keep from being the scapegoat.	• Share information versus waste energy on defending themselves.
• Punish the "guilty," as if that will solve the problem.	• Keep people posted on the process so they know the issue is being addressed.
• Ruin relationships, inhibit trust, and impede workflow.	• Build relationships and learn.

QUESTIONS TO ASK YOURSELF

- Is the need to be right important to me? (Think about this one. It's not easy to admit.)
- Am I aware of the current language I use in problem solving? Could my word choice or tone be interpreted as blaming?

- If *The Blame Game* is being played in my organization, how can I discuss its impact on teamwork and productivity with my leadership team or those I lead?
- In what ways do I model *The Take Responsibility and Be Accountable Game*?

YOUR CHALLENGE

1. Rate yourself on your current use of **Real Power # 1: Create a Safe, Collaborative Environment**

    _____ I need to develop
    _____ I do fairly well
    _____ I'm totally skilled

2. For the next few days, notice which game is being played in your organization: *The Blame Game* or *The Take Responsibility and Be Accountable Game*. Assess how *The Blame Game* may be inhibiting results. Note if and where *The Take Responsibility and Be Accountable Game* is being played and how that is working. Which game do you want to encourage your team to play? How will you do that?

3. How can you apply **Real Power #1** to increase your own leadership effectiveness?

CHAPTER 6

YOUR TEAM CAN'T READ YOUR MIND

You can't talk your way out of what you've behaved yourself into.
—Stephen R. Covey

It's not unusual for leaders to *think* they communicate their expectations clearly, behave in ways they *believe* support what they say they want, and then be surprised to discover that their messages miss the mark completely. From their employees' point of view, the leader appears to be sending mixed and inconsistent messages.

Often leaders unknowingly expect their direct reports to know what they are thinking and can be totally unaware of how their own behavior *doesn't* support what they say they want. As a leader, your credibility is at stake when your words, actions, and expectations aren't in alignment.

Real Power #2:
Align Your Expectations, Words and Actions

Don's Story: "Daddy" Don

As Don, a director of marketing, expressed it, "I want my team to act independently and not run to me for approval on every little thing." He told me he felt like "Daddy" Don because his team members were always flagging him down to ask questions that he thought they should be able to figure out for themselves. He assumed his team knew what he wanted from them. His frustration showed in his tone of voice, his impatience, his abruptness in ending a conversation, and his absence when they needed his input. His intent, he said, was to build his team's creativity and self-reliance.

When interviewed, here's what Don's team said: "He never says no to a project that he is requested to do! He throws too many projects over the wall to us and expects us to run with them. He doesn't appear to value us, since he never does a thorough handoff so that we can be successful. *Then* he disappears, and we take exorbitant amounts of time to backtrack and find out what was promised to our customers. Often we don't have a clue what he has in mind, so we have to try to sit him down long enough to get that information—but he's hard to find."

Rather than building his team's creativity and self-reliance, which was Don's sincere desire, his behavior was creating exactly the opposite: his team needed him more than ever. Hearing this feedback, Don had to explore how his expectations, his behavior, and the actual impact he was having were totally out of alignment. As a result, he could see that he might be a large part of his own problem and was willing to take responsibility for making some changes.

Don's Discoveries

After some coaching, Don realized how the incongruent dynamic he had set up was affecting the entire group's effectiveness and ability to meet the company's high standards. With further exploration into his own beliefs, Don discovered a surprising "payoff" he received for his elusive behavior—with his staff constantly trying to get his attention, he could feel "wanted" and "in demand." When that payoff became clear, Don decided the ego boost wasn't worth the frustration he had created.

Don also saw that he was playing to his strengths of getting creative projects for his team, while avoiding his weaker area of getting involved in the details. He realized his black-and-white thinking had him sidestepping the details completely, or getting swallowed up in them, with nothing in between. He was clear that he needed to check with his group on the impact of potential new projects and do a complete handoff so *they* could deal with the details effectively.

We set up a few team meetings in which Don addressed this issue openly. Don and his marketing team defined and agreed on guidelines that would stimulate the creativity and self-reliance that were his true intent. The team, it turned out, wanted the same outcome, and now they could align with him and pursue the goal together.

COACHING RECOMMENDATIONS

Don's lack of alignment between what he *said* he wanted, the fact that he never clearly articulated his expectation to his team, and his *behavior* is not unusual for a leader. But it does provide some important points to consider about your own leadership:

- If your direct reports aren't acting the way you think they should, stop the action and check out why. Be curious. Don't make them wrong.
- Consider that your teams' unexpected behavior may be a direct reflection of your leadership: something you are doing (or not doing). Check it out.
- Ask yourself whether you're sending congruent messages about what you expect. Identify where you are, or are not, being clear and consistent.
- Set your employees up to succeed—which guidelines, meetings, permission, and protocols do they need to have in place to achieve success in their jobs?
- Define and communicate what you need from them; tell them your expectations. Then listen to what they need from you. Agree to what you will do and explain what you won't do. Get the same clarity from them on what they agree to do and not do.

Stop and Get Feedback

As you work on aligning your expectations, words, and actions, getting consistent feedback is important. You can start with a self-check by asking yourself: "I am intending X. Are my followers getting that clear message in my words and actions? Do I see, in their responses and actions, that they understand my expectations? Does my ongoing behavior support what I'm saying I want?"

To validate your self-check, get feedback from those you lead. Remember, Don thought he was doing everything right.

As in the case of "Daddy" Don, you actually *gain* power by pausing, getting real-time feedback, and then looking at your own behavior first. Your behavior is the one thing over which you have complete control. Often, simple, conscious changes in your actions and in what you communicate are all that is required to get things back on track and to boost your leadership effectiveness to a higher level.

HOW YOU KNOW WHEN YOU ARE
Out of Alignment

- Like "Daddy" Don, you feel frustrated and disappointed that your people aren't performing in a certain way, or perhaps that your intentions have been misinterpreted, or that you aren't getting the results you expected.
- You feel you are doing everything you can to communicate your expectations—and you just don't understand what the problem could be.
- You find yourself thinking: "What's *wrong* with these people?"

QUESTIONS TO ASK YOURSELF

- Am I clear that my credibility is at risk if what I say, do, and expect of my team aren't in alignment?
- Could I be sending conflicting messages to my team that I am not aware of?
- Would those I lead agree that I am communicating my expectations clearly?
- Do I regularly ask for feedback to confirm that I am aligned in what I say, do, and expect? If so, what does the feedback tell me?
- How can I change my own behavior first?

YOUR CHALLENGE

1. Rate yourself on your current use of *Real* **Power # 2:**
   Align Your Expectations, Words, and Actions

   ____ I need to develop
   ____ I do fairly well
   ____ I'm totally skilled

2. Identify an area within your team where things don't seem to be going as well as you would like. Explore what might be causing the disconnect between what you expect and what is actually happening. Ask questions of those involved to gain insight into how they see the situation. Don't attempt to "fix" anything until you have gathered all the pieces of the puzzle. Consider asking someone else to gather the feedback for you. When you have completed your discovery process, you'll be in a better position to take action. Be open to the fact that things may be off track because you need to communicate your expectations and then back them up with consistent and congruent words and actions.

3. How can you apply *Real* **Power #2** to increase your own leadership effectiveness?

CHAPTER 7

PUT SOME WALK IN YOUR TALK

*Example is not the main thing in influencing others,
it is the only thing.*
—Albert Schweitzer

"Do as I say, not as I do" is a formula for disaster in today's workplace. Leaders who act as if their position exempts them from all the rules they impose and the behavior they expect of others will soon find that they are cultivating resentment and distrust.

Real leadership power is earned, not dictated. You can guide others by showing them the way. Remember that the positive impact of your Leadership Force Field begins with your own character and behavior.

Real Power #3:
Model What You Expect of Others

Brian, Scott, Julie, and Steve—
Misjudge Their Impact

Brian was a leader who did not answer e-mails. His employees would send him several, and then give up after getting no response. Yet when Brian needed something, he would send urgent e-mails and expect immediate responses. His employees would scramble to get him the information he requested. When Brian's emergency had been handled, he would go back to not answering e-mails—until the next time he needed something.

> **Brian's rationale:** I'm the boss. They should respond to me quickly. If I answered everyone's emails as soon as I received them, I'd never get anything else done.

> **Impact:** Brian's staff resented the lack of reciprocity in his e-mail practice. They had no way of knowing if he even read their e-mails or received important messages they sent. They were unsure about how to get Brian's attention. Time was wasted attempting to contact him, and they weren't as confident moving forward without his acknowledgment or input.

Scott, a leader of a large organization, never showed up for his staff meetings on time, yet he expected everyone to be there waiting for him.

> **Scott's rationale:** My schedule is busier than their schedules. They understand the importance of my role.

> **Impact:** Over time, others throughout Scott's organization felt their schedules were too busy to be on time for *their* meetings. As a result, too much meeting time

was wasted waiting for people to show up. In Scott's organization, the unspoken, unproductive norm was: "being late = I'm important."

Julie required detailed quarterly reports from her staff. She made a commitment to combine the information, publish the compiled data, and discuss it with her direct reports so that they would have a clear, up-to-date understanding of what was going on in their organization. She rarely did so.

Julie's rationale: I need their data to report to my boss.

Impact: Julie's staff mimicked her behavior by making commitments they also did not keep, including their commitments to her. "Do what you say you will do" had spotty application throughout their entire department.

Steve had an explosive temper and was known as a bully. He had no tolerance for mistakes or delays.

Steve's rationale: This is the way I am, and I'm the boss.

Impact: Steve's staff walked on eggshells for fear of Steve's wrath. Many topics went undiscussed. Some other leaders copied his behavior to appear powerful.

Each of these leaders assumed they were exempt from the rules of fair play. None of them were tuned in to the long-term impact they were having. Think of a time you had a leader like Brian, Scott, Julie, or Steve. Did behavior like this from your leader communicate that you were valued and respected? How did it cause you problems with getting your own job done? Did you feel resentment? How did it affect your willingness to go the extra mile for him or her?

COACHING RECOMMENDATIONS

Like it or not, organizations become reflections of their leaders, and people take their cues from your behavior. That's why it is so important for you to be aware of what you do and the impact you are having. You want to be sure that who you are being, and what you say and do, are what you want to see reflected throughout your organization.

Integrity and credibility are built through your everyday actions. So is resentment. It is essential to know whether you are perceived as "walking your talk" or instead have fallen into the trap of believing "rank has its privileges."

You always have a choice about the behavior you model for those you lead. You can be a warning to others or you can be an inspiration. Effective leadership is about inspiring others to be the best they can be by being the best that *you* can be.

Get Feedback

Since we can't always see ourselves as others see us, knowing whether or not you are perceived as walking your talk requires feedback from others.

Treat feedback as a navigational tool. You wouldn't drive a car or fly a plane without checking your gauges: speed, oil, tire pressure, and fuel. Feedback is an essential factor in successfully navigating your leadership territory.

If there are qualities you expect in your employees, it's important to know if you are perceived as demonstrating those same qualities. By gathering the feedback and working on areas in which you may not exactly shine, you are also modeling a powerful process of constantly working to improve your value as a leader.

How to Ask for Feedback

1. Check Your Mind-Set
The best mind-set for gathering feedback is *open and curious*. Park your ego on the sidelines. Be neutral and sincere.

2. Determine Whom to Ask for Feedback
You can request feedback from your boss, a trusted peer, someone who works for you, or all three. Each will provide you with a different perspective, which can be very illuminating. Select people who have observed you in action and can provide you with specific examples to help clarify their comments.

3. Be Specific
For example: "Terry, I trust your opinion and I'd like your perspective. I'm checking to see how I'm coming across. Are there some areas of my leadership where I could be perceived as not walking my talk? Especially in the area of respecting others? Do you have some specific examples for me about what you've observed directly? Any suggestions for how I can do things differently?"

4. Listen
Make sure you understand the feedback completely. Repeat back what you think you heard—for example, "So when I don't respond to e-mails I receive from them, my team thinks that I don't respect them and am not interested in supporting them? And the impact is that their work gets held up waiting for my input? Did I hear that correctly?"

5. Drop Your Defense

Don't argue or defend your behavior with the person giving you the feedback. It takes courage to listen openly and with curiosity, especially when it's about you. You stop listening when you start justifying your own actions. Arguing or defending yourself will also make it less likely for people to give you honest feedback in the future.

6. Express Appreciation

Thank the people who give you feedback. It's risky to give feedback, especially if you are their boss. Their biggest fear is that they will upset you or experience future retaliation for their honesty. Let them know their information is appreciated and confidential.

7. Respond Constructively

Do something with the feedback you receive. Try a new approach. Let your team members know what you are working on, and ask for their support and cooperation. And never retaliate for feedback you find hard to take. Validate feedback you find surprising with others, and if you get similar feedback, you would be wise to pay attention.

Use a Neutral Third Party

Often a neutral third party can get better feedback for you than you could gather yourself. Hire a leadership coach or use internal resources to help you get the feedback you would like to have.
A coach or neutral third party can do the following:

- Interview others to gather specific feedback for you
- Observe you in action and give you unbiased feedback
- Clarify the feedback so that you know what do differently
- Support and guide you in making any necessary changes

Feedback Is a Gift

Over time, how you request and respond to feedback can open up the channels of communication in your organization. People will get used to giving thoughtful, useful input and appreciate that you are listening to them. You can then calibrate what is working and not working in how you operate as a leader, and be able to make effective changes.

HOW YOU KNOW WHEN YOU AREN'T
Walking Your Talk

You may not be walking your talk if feedback (whether formal, informal, or through the company grapevine) tells you that you aren't being perceived as the kind of leader you think you are or aspire to be.

QUESTIONS TO ASK YOURSELF

- If I see behaviors in my organization that are not what I'd like to see, am I willing to look at how they may be a reflection of my own behavior?
- Am I willing to get feedback from others to validate how I walk my talk as a leader? Am I willing to make changes based on that feedback?
- How can I involve the whole team in discussing the qualities and actions I want to model as a leader and see replicated throughout our team?

YOUR CHALLENGE

1. Rate yourself on your current use of ***Real* Power #3**:
   Model What You Expect of Others

   _____ I need to develop
   _____ I do fairly well
   _____ I'm totally skilled

2. Think of one quality or behavior you expect of your team. For example: having a sense of humor, doing what they say they will do, responding promptly to requests, or something else you value. Then ask three people how they think you model that characteristic for your team. Ask your boss, a trusted peer, and someone who works for you. Ask them one-on-one and in private. Be focused but keep the conversation informal.

   Pay attention to your own behavior around asking for feedback. Follow the guidelines under "How to Ask for Feedback," above. Collect the feedback and see if it is consistent. Would you say that you are walking your talk in that area, or do you have some work to do? Was the feedback you gathered specific enough so that you know what to do differently? Can you see ways of gathering feedback in the future that can be frequent, informal, and useful to you?

3. How can you apply ***Real* Power #3** to increase your own leadership effectiveness?

CHAPTER 8

WHAT'S IN YOUR RELATIONSHIP BANK ACCOUNT?

If the only time someone sees you is when you want something, then you're not going to build a strong relationship.
—David Maister

Step back and think about how work gets done: it's through and with people. As a leader, the bigger your network, the wider your range of influence—and the more you can remove obstacles and build support for projects and people you lead. If the balance in your Relationship Bank Account is low, you can also count on your influence, collaboration, and support being low. People work best with people they know and trust.

Real Power #4:
Build a Relationship Network

Jeff's Story

Jeff, a VP of business development, was surprised by feedback he received on his annual leadership assessment. He was rated very low in peer relationships and having influence outside of his own department. In interviews I conducted to gather more detailed information for him, Jeff's boss said that he focused exclusively on his team and wasn't noticing the impact he was having on his peers or on other departments with whom his group interfaced.

His boss explained that Jeff was gaining a reputation for being hard to deal with. There was also consensus among Jeff's peers that he couldn't be trusted. If Jeff wanted to be successful, he would need to open up the scope of his leadership and start paying attention to other leaders and other parts of the organization.

Building Relationships or Playing Politics?

When I discussed this feedback with Jeff, he defended himself, saying that he had no time for "politics" and did not want to play. He saw developing relationships outside of his immediate department as time-consuming, manipulative, and distracting. He had seen too many people play politics, to the detriment of their real work, and that wasn't going to be his story.

In Jeff's mind, building relationships and playing politics were intertwined. I asked him to describe what "being political" looked like to him. He answered that being political meant being dishonest, looking good but not creating true value, and pushing narrow or personal interests. It would involve faking friendship just to get what he wanted. I confirmed that he had described the dark side of relationship building—and not what he was being asked to do.

The truth about his definition is that organizations, by their very nature, are a complex maze of egos and issues, with some people out for their own self-interest. Jeff had seen people manipulate relationships for their own advantage and didn't like it. Maintaining his integrity, ethics, and values as he navigated his own organizational maze would be the key to avoiding his current definition of "being political." Besides, I reminded him, he was *not* playing politics now, yet feedback from his boss and peers described him as "difficult and not trustworthy." What was wrong with this picture?

Jeff could see that continuing to avoid what he called "playing politics" was not going to change how he was perceived. He wanted to be viewed as he felt he was—honest, dedicated, and focused. It was, however, becoming clear to him that *something* needed to change. He just wasn't sure what he could do or would be willing to do.

Why Building Relationships Makes Sense

Jeff would benefit from reexamining his definitions of influence, building relationships, and playing politics. Without some clear distinctions, he would most likely be unable to make any significant changes in his thinking and behavior.

I asked Jeff to listen to two descriptions of hypothetical colleagues:

- Colleague #1 has listened to you, supported many of your ideas, diverted some resources to you, and at times asked for your support. You also meet each other for coffee and informal conversations. You understand her thinking and what's important to her, and vice versa. When you have differing points of view, you hear each other out and often agree to disagree.
- Colleague #2 is someone you see only at meetings you both attend. Your groups interface and work on joint projects, but you let your direct reports handle the interactions. You have never spent any time with this colleague outside of formal

meetings. You don't know anything else about him except that he can be forceful when selling his own ideas. He shows no interest in you or what's happening in your area of the company.

Then I asked Jeff which colleague he would be most likely to trust. With whom would he be most likely to collaborate? Which person would have the most ability to influence him, and which one could he most likely influence?

Jeff answered that he would definitely find it easier to trust and work with Colleague #1. Trying to have a conversation with Colleague #2, without an existing relationship in place, could be difficult. It might even end up feeling manipulative, since they would probably be talking only when they needed something from each other. He felt that he might not be able to trust Colleague #2, since he didn't know him as well as Colleague #1. Jeff also admitted that his own behavior was more like that of Colleague #2. He wondered if that might be why his peers felt they couldn't trust him.

Jeff Expands His Leadership Territory

I asked Jeff what he could gain by expanding his relationships beyond his own team. He thought about it a minute, and said, "It would be better if I built relationships before I need them. Building trust and opening up communications requires that people get to know me and that I get to know my peers. I am trustworthy, and I want people to know that about me. I couldn't believe they wouldn't trust me until I experienced how I felt about Colleague #2 in your example. I didn't know him so I didn't trust him."

Jeff paused thoughtfully, then continued, "I'm always complaining about how we all seem to work in 'silos,' duplicating work and not knowing what other groups are working on. Now I can see how

I might be contributing to that situation by staying so focused on just what my team is doing."

Jeff was beginning to realize that what he had rejected as political and unnecessary was, in fact, a key part of his job. To be a more effective leader, he would need to build a network of relationships in ways that supported both his own values and his sincere desire to do the best for his team.

Making Deposits in His Relationship Bank Account

To give Jeff another image to work with, I asked him to think of building relationships as making investments. I call them "deposits" in a Relationship Bank. If you have more deposits than withdrawals, you are managing the balance and exchange well. You most likely understand what others need and have built a certain level of familiarity and trust with them. You have money in the bank.

However, if you make no deposits and expect to make withdrawals, you will soon find that you are bankrupt. People will see you as always out for your own self-interest and not terribly concerned with what might be important to them.

A particularly important element of this exchange is that the Relationship Bank and its transactions are about people. So you need to truly value people and see them as an important aspect of work. You always have a dual focus: task *and* relationship. Always. It's the commitment you work from, every day.

Develop a Relationship Action Plan

With his new commitment to building relationships before he needed them, Jeff was ready to go into action. He decided to request and schedule meetings with his peers and key people in other departments. He thought that lunch or coffee meetings with one person each week, for the first few months, would get his relationship building commitment launched. Then he could set up a regular touch-base schedule after that. For those at other locations, he would work them into his travel schedule or arrange a phone conversation.

Jeff Plans His First Meetings

Jeff would explain to each person that his agenda for the meeting was to find out how things were going in their areas and to explore building a more collaborative relationship between their departments and themselves. He wanted to understand what was important to them, what their biggest challenges were, and how they might work better together.

Jeff also wanted them to know a little more about him and his team, but he would make that about 10 percent of the conversation, devoting 90 percent to learning more about *them*. Jeff set an intention that they would see him as confident, genuine, collaborative, and willing to expand his leadership to include important relationships with other leaders.

I reminded Jeff to focus on *building a relationship* with each person, not just having a regular work discussion focused on a businesslike exchange of information. His goal was to develop a *personal connection* that would create a basis for trust and set a positive framework for future communications.

Jeff thought the questions he prepared would help to keep a good balance of business and personal aspects to the meeting. He agreed to listen and watch for any personal interests they might share— for example, music, sports, recreational activities, favorite travel destinations, causes they supported, and so on.

With the help of his assistant, Jeff's meetings were scheduled. He didn't want to go on autopilot and just get these meetings checked off his list. He sincerely wanted to know if he was making progress. By debriefing his meetings with me, he had time committed to reflect on what he was learning and the kind of impact he was having.

So What Were Jeff's Results?

After six months, Jeff requested that I do some follow-up interviews with his peers to see if he was making progress. Everyone I interviewed felt they knew Jeff better and thought he was more cooperative and easier to talk to. They gave him high marks for all that he was doing to change his image and build relationships across departments. When asked if they felt they could trust him, they all responded, "Yes, much more than before." That was exactly what Jeff wanted to hear.

Jeff realized that what he had started was the beginning of an ongoing commitment and process that he would need to maintain. He was surprised by how easy it was when he put building relationships on his priority list and got appointments scheduled on his calendar. He even found himself making better use of random time that he had with his colleagues before and after meetings. He made a point of connecting, in some way, to replenish his Relationship Bank Accounts.

In our coaching sessions over the next year, Jeff reported that he understood his colleagues' points of view much better, and they also understood his better. He thought that his efforts had created a much-improved context for getting work done. As he expanded his Relationship Network throughout the organization, he found himself having access to more information. He felt that he had people's attention if he made a request or voiced a suggestion.

He had replaced his resistance to "playing politics" with a desire to "be known and trusted."

Jeff had changed as a leader in a way that was even *more* in line with the value he wanted to provide for his team. He also felt that it expanded his personal job satisfaction when he had supportive colleagues who could discuss issues more openly within trusting relationships.

COACHING RECOMMENDATIONS

Relationship building has to be as intentional and important as getting other work results. Do something to build and connect with your network every day. Once again, an effective leader focuses on task *and* relationship, not one or the other. Does it take time? Yes. Is it an investment that will pay back with dividends? Absolutely.

HOW YOU KNOW WHEN YOU MAY NOT BE
Building A Network

- Like, Jeff, you think that building relationships throughout the organization is time-consuming, merely playing politics, or just a distraction from getting "real work" done. So you don't do it.
- You spend all your time with your own team.
- You get feedback that tells you people don't really know you, your team, or what value either of you contributes.
- Other leaders don't appear to trust you and are suspicious of your motives.
- You don't know much about your peers and colleagues. You have no idea what value they create and what they are trying to accomplish.

QUESTIONS TO ASK YOURSELF

- Can I think of times when having strong relationships outside of my immediate team helped me to get things done or have my ideas considered?
- How is my Relationship Bank Account? Full and active, bankrupt, or somewhere in between?
- How do I balance task *and* relationship on my leadership agenda?
- Do I believe that taking the time to build relationships will make me a better leader? Why or why not?

YOUR CHALLENGE

1. Rate yourself on your current use of *Real* **Power #4:**
   Build a Relationship Network

   _____ I need to develop
   _____ I do fairly well
   _____ I'm totally skilled

2. Think about your strategy for building critical relationships within and outside of your team, department, and organization. Do you have one? Check your calendar. Do you have meetings scheduled to keep your Relationship Bank Account full?

   Make a list of three key people you would like to get to know better. Set up a coffee, lunch, or after-work meeting. Or make an appointment to have a meeting in their office. Be prepared to ask questions and to share both professional and personal information.

   Notice your comfort level and how you manage the conversation. Write down what you learn about each person after your meeting. How will you continue to keep making deposits in each of your three new Relationship Bank Accounts? Notice how knowing more about these people creates a better context for getting work done.

3. How can you apply **Real Power #4** to increase your own leadership effectiveness?

THE INTROVERT'S RELATIONSHIP BANK ACCOUNT

Introverts often face the biggest challenge when dealing with the relationship building part of leadership. They prefer one-on-one interactions to group events and will build close friendships with a few people. Having lots of friends or relationships isn't their goal. They seek quality over quantity. As leaders, though, they find that the demands for building numerous relationships increase.

Introverts rarely enjoy the small talk required in group situations, they value work over conversation *about* work, and they have difficulty with the amount of energy it takes to relate to a larger number of people. Often, during busy workdays, relationships are not even on their radar screens. It's the way they are wired. So can those who are naturally introverted be successful at relationship building? Yes. Introverts just need to make a plan.

If developing relationships is not a native skill, balancing your Relationship Bank Account will take forethought. Plan and regularly schedule dates on your calendar for one-on-one "get to know you meetings" with other leaders. Prepare and craft questions to help you learn about the other person, his or her challenges, and how you might be of assistance or how your respective teams could better interface or collaborate. Discover some interests that you share outside of work. Make a plan to build relationships one step at a time and work your plan.

Targeting and Managing Your Energy

If introverts come to see how relationship-building interactions forward the action, they can often push past their natural discomfort with the process. At one point, I coached Bruce, a VP of a high-tech company and an introvert, to prepare for a four-day executive offsite he dreaded each year. As a result of our work together, he had a plan and ended up being surprised by what a productive, enjoyable time he had. He also had a strategy for all future events, which he had a history of avoiding.

Bruce first identified a specific overall outcome he wanted to achieve: "I want to leave this offsite with the following information/insight/connections... *and* make the following impression about me and my team with my colleagues...."

He planned whom he strategically needed to talk to and whether he wanted to set up a future meeting with them. He thought through his questions carefully about topics on which he wanted to probe other leaders' perspectives. He also prepared key statements about what he wanted other people to know about his top priorities and his group's contribution to the bigger picture.

Bruce was relieved when I asked him to schedule time to be alone to process his thoughts, and also time to rest from the stress of being with so many people. He knew if he tried to keep up with all of the social activities and the meetings, as he usually demanded of himself, he would be exhausted, both mentally and physically.

After creating a plan that supported his introverted style, Bruce was eager to attend the executive offsite. With his preparation and new mind-set, his previous feelings of dread and overwhelm no longer became a self-fulfilling prophecy.

CHAPTER 9

WHAT MESSAGES ARE YOU *REALLY* SENDING?

*The single biggest problem in communication
is the illusion that it has taken place.*
—George Bernard Shaw

Do you know how you come across in your everyday conversations? Are you optimizing the moments when you are in direct contact with your employees, colleagues, customers, and others? Do you continue to inspire others in those less formal interactions?

Informal conversations are often just as powerful as your prepared presentations in reinforcing the key messages you want to send. Be conscious of the messages you are sending as you speak to people every day.

Real Power #5 :
Optimize Your Daily, Informal Communications

You Are *Always* Communicating

Research tells us that only 10 percent of our message is conveyed through our words. The other 90 percent is communicated through our tone (45 percent) plus our body language (45 percent). This is why e-mails and text messages can provide information and clarity but aren't the ideal vehicle for all communication. People still test for authenticity by hearing our tone and seeing our body language. And if body language accounts for 45 percent of any communication, it explains how we can be communicating even when we are *listening*.

Being aware of the subtle signals sent by your word choice, tone, and body language gives you an opportunity to change communication habits you have that may be sabotaging your intended messages.

Words Are 10 Percent of Your Message

Words have the ability to inspire people to do their best, or to create self-consciousness and uncertainty. It's important to consider the words you choose to express yourself and the impact those words may be having.

One leader told me that whenever conflict arises, she asks her team, "How can we work through this issue and keep our team intact?" Another leader uses different words: "If there is a conflict of interest, fight it out among yourselves." These leaders' choice of words reveals their different beliefs about conflict and sends different messages to their teams.

Some leaders use negative words to communicate: "We can't afford to fail. They may outsource our department if we do." Others use positive words: "Let's demonstrate why we are the top performers and exceed their expectations."

Focus on What You Want

Linguistic studies tell us that using words that focus on what we *want* instead of what we *don't want* directs the focus of our listeners in a more productive direction. You may have done this exercise before, but here goes: "*Don't* think of a red pencil." What's the first thing you think of? Most likely, it's a red pencil. Do you wonder why you think of a red pencil when I asked you not to? The brain actually cancels out the "do not or don't" and hears the message: "red pencil." So now imagine yelling, "Don't fall!" to a mountain climber; "Don't crash!" to a pilot; "Don't make a mistake" to your assistant; or "Don't jump in that puddle!" to a four-year-old. Where are you directing their attention?

Using words that express what you *do* want instead of what you *don't* want stimulates thinking and creates a positive focus that is more aligned with achieving your desired behavior and outcomes. Tune in to the words you use as you talk to employees every day. Do the words you choose encourage, support, inspire, and focus on what you want? Or do you unintentionally use words that are critical, negative, or describe what you don't want?

Body Language Is 45 Percent of Your Message

One leader was described as "sucking all the air out of the room" and "taking up all the space." His presence was large and loud. His employees felt there wasn't much room for them in any meeting he attended. He dominated the space and the agenda.

Another leader had such an intense stare when she listened that her staff described it as having "the ability to burn a hole through us and make us squirm in discomfort." They thought her face communicated that she was listening to criticize and judge rather than listening with an open mind.

Yet another seasoned leader listened with her arms crossed, made no eye contact, waited a short time for her direct report to speak, and then leaned forward, pointing her finger at the person as she spoke. Her employees experienced her as parental and directive.

Since body language makes up 45 percent of your total communication, becoming aware of it and the messages it sends makes sense. You can also see from the examples that your body language continues to communicate, even when you are *listening*. Direct feedback from people you work with is key to understanding how you come across.

Change Your Body Language, Change Your Message

Here's how two of these leaders listened to the feedback they received and made some positive changes.

The leader who "sucked all the air out of the room" was a very enthusiastic, confident person who loved his work. He also loved being the center of attention. Since he was always focused on what was best for the company, he felt his large presence was motivating and inspiring. And to a certain extent, he was right. His employees valued his expertise and enthusiasm. However, they also felt overshadowed, with no space for their ideas and questions.

Taking his feedback to heart, this leader learned to tone down his presence and not the enthusiasm level of his employees.

He announced that he heard their feedback and would be making some changes in his behavior. At meetings, he no longer took the seat at the head of the table. By sitting on the side in a middle seat, he reminded himself (and communicated to his team) that he wanted to be more of a "guide on the side" in meetings, as opposed to taking up all the space. He listened more and got a better sense of what his team was thinking. His team members, in turn, were able to contribute their own ideas and felt their meetings were more balanced and productive.

The leader whose concentrated stare burned a hole through her employees' self-confidence *thought* she was coming across as focused and concerned. She was stunned to discover that her employees experienced her thoughtful listening as critical and judgmental. She had no idea that anyone would see her as anything but sincere. With practice, she learned how to soften her facial expressions while listening.

She also learned that it was difficult to modify her facial expressions, since she had listened that way all her life. She decided to simply tell people that when she listened, she did so with an intensity that might look like criticism. What they needed to know was that she was really listening deeply and not thinking negatively about what they were saying. Her upfront explanation helped others to interpret her stern look more comfortably and improved her communications with everyone.

Check Your Body Language Communication

Body language is subtle, often below our level of conscious awareness, but still communicating in a powerful way. The first step in checking what your own body language may be communicating is to get feedback. Ask people you trust and who see you in action to tell you how you come across in daily scenarios. You can also work with a coach and have yourself video recorded in a meeting. Seeing yourself in action can be life changing. The gaps between how we *think* we act, the way we *actually* express ourselves, and the *impact* we have on others is often a surprising revelation.

Tone of Voice Is 45 Percent of Your Message

Emphasis and tone change meaning. Read the following statements out loud, with the emphasis on the italicized words:

1. What were you thinking? (genuinely curious tone)
2. **What** were you thinking? (incredulous tone)
3. **What were you thinking!** (angry tone)

Can you imagine how tone and emphasis load those same words with different meanings? Your tone will communicate what you are really thinking, as well as the emotional intensity of what you are feeling.

One leader was so focused on task and results that he used his voice and comments to "whip people into action," as he expressed it. He spoke abruptly and quickly, with a sharp tone. He wanted to energize and speed up the activity.

Another leader used a skeptical, disbelieving tone to validate any data that was presented to him. His intention was to be thorough and accurate. He simply wanted people to "prove it to him." He wanted to be convinced that their data was solid. His direct reports, though, found him "very critical and quick to question our facts." They had difficulty communicating their ideas when he "doubted everything we said."

Another leader joked and was sarcastic. She thought she was being funny. Her employees had difficulty deciphering what she really meant.

Your tone of voice, representing 45 percent of your total communication, can change your message completely. Here again, you need direct feedback to understand how your tone may be undermining or supporting you.

Your tone may be habitual: you've always talked that way, people in your family always talked that way, a former boss talked that way. Regardless, you won't hear it yourself, so you need feedback. You can record yourself during phone conversations and as you participate in meetings. Or ask a trusted colleague to listen specifically for your tone of voice and the impact she notices it having. Request that she give you some honest feedback on what she observed.

COACHING RECOMMENDATIONS

You might consider your choice of words, your body language and your tone of voice to be trivial when you are concerned with much bigger issues. However, if you intend to move up the leadership ranks, those subtle little things begin to count more and more to differentiate exceptional leaders from the rest of the contenders for top leadership positions.

Keep in mind that this chapter refers to *informal* conversations, the ones for which you don't usually prepare—the ones you have every day.

Here are some guidelines and checkpoints for your informal conversations:

- **Be Congruent from the Core.** Your beliefs, thinking, and intentions must first be congruent so that the external expression of them will also be congruent. Imagine the impact of trying to come across as collaborative when you have a strong belief that playing *The Blame Game* keeps people motivated and competitive. In this case, your choice of words, your tone, and your body language would most likely reflect your *true* beliefs and undermine the message you think you are sending about collaboration. If you don't believe in what you are saying, you can bet those listening will get *that* message loud and clear.

- **Get Feedback from Others.** Since our communication styles are largely habitual, some kind of external feedback is absolutely essential. Seek out highly specific feedback from people with whom you work. Ask them how you come across in your day-to-day communications. Ask about your words, your tone of voice, and your body language. Ask them for adjectives they think best describe you as a communicator. Is that how you want to be described? If so, keep doing what you are doing, but continue checking in with them. If not, what can you do differently to send congruent and credible messages?

- **A Picture Is Still Worth a Thousand Words.** Arrange to video record a meeting or some other scenario in which you are interacting with others. If you can actually see yourself as others see you, then you can decide whether your words, tone, and body language are all congruent with the message you want to send. You may also benefit from having your coach view the video with you to point out things you may not see.

HOW YOU KNOW WHEN YOU ARE NOT
Optimizing Your Daily, Informal Communications

- You sometimes get feedback that doesn't match your own self-assessment of how you come across as a leader in your everyday interactions.
- You don't even think about how you are coming across in your everyday, informal communications.
- You are too busy to *care* how you are coming across every day in your informal interactions with employees, colleagues, and others in your organization.

QUESTIONS TO ASK YOURSELF

- Am I aware of the importance of my informal communications?
- How would I know if my words, tone, and body language were sending a congruent message, or not? How could I find out?

YOUR CHALLENGE

1. Rate yourself on your current use of **Real Power #5: Optimize Your Daily, Informal Communications**

 _____ I need to develop
 _____ I do fairly well
 _____ I'm totally skilled

2. Start with a self-check of your everyday, informal communications. Tune in and listen to yourself for one day, or even *one* informal conversation, this week. Are the words you choose, your tone, and your body language congruent with who you want to be as a leader? Are you sending the messages in your informal, daily conversations that you truly want to send?

Do your words encourage, support, inspire, and focus on what you want? Or do they consistently analyze, criticize, and create uncertainty? Does your tone affect your intended meaning? Does your body language send a conflicting message? For example, do you think you are being attentive and respectful to a colleague who is sitting in your office talking to you while you are also reading your e-mail on your computer?

Observe how others react to what you say or do.

3. How can you apply ***Real* Power #5** to increase your own leadership effectiveness?

CHAPTER 10

BUILD BRIDGES, NOT CASTLES

*People don't care how much you know
until they know how much you care.*
— Theodore Roosevelt

Being remote and unapproachable might have worked for leaders in the past, but even in our technologically advanced world, there is no substitute for personal connection.

People need to know that they matter, and they are more likely to trust people they know. Building rapport with your team creates trust, connection and loyalty. A lack of rapport with your team can show up as resistance—and you might be completely unaware of the dynamic that is undermining you.

Real Power #6:
Maintain Rapport with the People You Lead

Lynn's Story

Lynn, a vice president in a biotech company, was a leader who demonstrated a natural ability for creating rapport. She explained it this way:

"Totally focusing on the tasks, the work, and the results only gets you so far. People want to do their best and they want to make a difference. Being in rapport with those you lead is much more than acknowledging their good work. It's tapping into that basic human need to be seen, included, valued, and to have a voice. I believe that connecting on a personal level with people is essential for a leader to lead anyone anywhere."

When I asked Lynn's staff what she did to build rapport, here's what they said: "Lynn checks in to see how we are doing and asks what she can do to help. She reminds us of the group's goals and how we are each an important part of the effort, and she means it. She steps out of her world into ours to see how things are going."

To understand how to build rapport, it's important to understand how rapport works—the essence of it. In South Africa, the Zulu greeting "*Sawubona*" means, "I see you." It simply acknowledges the basic human need to be seen by others. In our very busy world that is focused on speed and results, we often forget our humanness and the need we have to feel that we matter. Being seen and acknowledged may seem insignificant in the pursuit of results—but effective leaders know that it's essential to continue building rapport with people who achieve those results.

The nature of rapport is such that you don't just create rapport once and you are done. It's important to establish rapport with others from the beginning and continue to build it regularly, in some way. Once you grasp the essence and value of rapport, you will see ways you can create and maintain it. We'll explore some specific ideas here, but it's essential to understand that your efforts to build rapport must be genuine.

When Rapport Goes Out the Door

Several years ago, I attended an eight-day workshop on creativity in France. The two instructors were highly renowned in their fields, and participants had come from around the world to attend. Now, doesn't that sound like a framework for an amazing experience? That's what we all thought. But on day two, the participants gathered in the hotel lobby after dinner to talk about what was going wrong.

The instructors seemed to be focused solely on their own agenda, and we felt that we weren't included. They skipped over such things as finding out who was in the room and what experiences we brought to the party. They talked *at* us and then slipped out the sliding glass doors in the meeting room at the end of the day, avoiding any opportunity to engage with us.

At our meeting on the evening of day two, we decided to call them down to the lobby in hopes that they would join our conversation. We wanted to change the dynamics, believing that things could improve. They declined our invitation and told us that whoever didn't like the workshop could leave. We were shocked—they weren't at all interested in finding out what we thought. Stunned, we just sat there. We groused among ourselves, feeling completely discouraged. I was a successful consultant—why couldn't I rally and turn this thing around? I soon realized it was because the leaders weren't even listening and weren't remotely interested in turning *anything* around. We didn't seem to matter to them. The impact? We became a disempowered group.

Four people left the workshop the next day. The leaders said nothing. We started showing up late and leaving early. We stepped out of the room if we didn't want to do an exercise. No comment from the instructors. We couldn't even get their attention by being visibly disengaged. As a group, we struggled with what to request. We wanted them to pay attention to us, to see us and let us actively participate in our own learning experience. Our requests sounded almost juvenile. Since when did grown men and women have to ask for something so basic?

We decided to forge ahead and make the best of it. We were miserable but determined not to have traveled all this distance, and spent all that money, for nothing. We each had successful careers back home—yet something about this situation baffled us all.

The Moral of the Story

I share this story because I think it condensed into eight days what happens subtly in corporations over time when rapport does not exist between the leader and his or her team: a group of people shifts from a positive, highly invested mind-set to feeling discouraged and often become completely shut down—all due to the lack of that one key ingredient: *rapport with their leader.*

Rapport is like electricity: you can't see it, but you can tell when it's on and when it's off—and it powers everything. As a leader, it is important to know that a lack of rapport with your team, or members of your team, can show up as resistance or lack of caring and, often, you might not even understand the dynamic that is undermining you.

Rapport is subtle and is often the secret ingredient in your effectiveness as a leader. Those who do it well just do it naturally. Unfortunately, you don't get much guidance in checking to see if your rapport with your employees is a quart low. So you have to look for the indicators yourself.

I have watched dynamics on teams and in organizations change dramatically when a leader puts attention, energy, and right action on *genuinely* building rapport. Trust is created when you develop rapport with the people you lead. It's another example of subtle actions creating powerful outcomes.

You might be wondering if the leaders of the creativity workshop in France ever realized how discouraged the group was and shifted their approach. No, they did not. I wrote a letter to them after the workshop to describe my experience and my disappointment. My letter was returned—unopened. I guess when you don't care— you *really* don't care.

Leadership Actions That Build Rapport

Here is a sample of how employees I have interviewed describe what it's like to be in rapport with their leader.

My leader does the following:

- Knows my strengths and what I can best contribute
- Makes eye contact and genuinely acknowledges me
- Knows a few personal things about me. For example: I have three kids and he asks how they are doing
- Stops by just to say hello and see how things are going with me
- Calls me or sends an e-mail asking for my perspective on an issue
- Values my contribution and lets me know that he does

- Keeps conversations between us confidential, and doesn't share information that we discuss in private without consulting me
- Shares some personal information about herself
- Listens with interest and complete attention when we talk
- Knows my name and addresses me by name

COACHING RECOMMENDATIONS

Rap•port *n: an emotional bond or friendly relationship between people based on mutual liking, trust, and a sense that they understand and share each other's concerns.*

As advanced as we get technologically, people are still the key component of any work environment. They want to know that they matter, and they are more likely to trust people they know. People will tap into their creativity and develop innovative solutions when they know their thoughts and ideas will be heard— when they feel there is a bridge of trust, connection, and understanding between themselves and their leaders.

The key challenge is understanding how important rapport is, and then keeping it high on your daily to-do list. Identify one rapport-building action you can take each day with your direct reports, your colleagues, and your boss. Notice the impact on the other person and his or her response. Keep in mind that these daily actions take little time and can consist of e-mails, voicemails, and short, personal check-ins to congratulate, acknowledge, thank, ask a question, or simply follow up on a previous conversation. Remember that you are building trust, connection, and loyalty every time you make the effort.

Sharing Information: How Much Is Just Right?

Some leaders feel that work is not the place for personal connections. They have resistance to sharing details about their personal lives. However, building rapport doesn't require sharing the intimate details of your life. Just share enough so that your employees can know more about you as a person.

I coached one leader whose team had no idea he had a family. They didn't know what he liked to do or where he went on vacation. They had no information with which to begin building a bridge of connection from their side of the relationship.

Another leader shared way too much. He made reference to the "exorbitant amount of money he was paid" and the exotic vacations he could afford to take. His openness actually created a huge gap between him and those not in his income bracket—which was most of his organization.

However, he neglected to share one thing that would have given others another insight into his world. He adopted greyhound dogs that had been involved in dog racing and were abandoned after their running years were over. He had about five of these dogs and supported agencies that worked to get greyhounds placed in adoptive homes. Sharing that would have shown an entirely different side of him with which people could have connected.

What you consider *small talk* can have a *big* impact. Think of what you would be comfortable sharing with your employees and share it. Keep in mind that people trust people they know. Isn't that true for you, too?

HOW YOU KNOW WHEN YOU
Lack Rapport

- People seem awkward or reserved around you. You might interpret it as respect, but it could also be that they lack connection with you as a person.
- You don't even *think* about how your people are doing, as long as they are getting their work done.
- You think business should be focused only on those activities that get results. Building rapport seems like socializing and a waste of time.
- You don't know anything about your employees, and they don't know much about you. Your personal life is completely private, and you believe they appreciate that same privacy.

QUESTIONS TO ASK YOURSELF

- What is it like when I am *in rapport* with someone? How does it affect my own behavior? Am I more willing to work with that person? Do I trust him or her more? Why?
- What tells me that I am *out of rapport* with someone? Does being out of rapport affect my willingness to trust that person? Do I know how to begin building rapport?
- Am I too busy to have a personal connection with people who work for me?
- Am I focused exclusively on task and results, above relationship?

YOUR CHALLENGE

1. Rate yourself on your current use of *Real* **Power #6:**
   Maintain Rapport with the People You Lead

   _____ I need to develop
   _____ I do fairly well
   _____ I'm totally skilled

2. Identify some simple things you could add to your daily schedule that would build rapport with the individuals on your team. If your team is geographically dispersed, how can you make that personal connection via e-mail and phone?

   Yes, you are busy, but remember that rapport lives in the small things: small actions on your part send the message that you "see" someone else. Even a wave across the cafeteria or a quick e-mail of thanks for a job well done can make someone feel acknowledged. Give it a try. Do it with sincerity, and you'll notice that you feel better as you boost confidence and connection with those you lead.

3. How can you apply *Real* **Power #6** to increase your own leadership effectiveness?

CHAPTER 11

ARE WE THERE YET?

Leaders must be close enough to relate to others,
but far enough ahead to motivate them.
—John Maxwell

When I ask leaders how often they talk to their direct reports about the big-picture context of their efforts, I usually get a response like: "They are all bright people. Telling them repeatedly about things they already know isn't necessary."

I have interviewed many teams, and too often their number one request of their leader is: "Talk to us. Tell us where we are now and how we are doing."

The reality is that bright people are hired to focus on their areas of expertise. They can easily lose sight of the bigger picture and where all the collective efforts are headed.

Real Power #7 :
Provide the Big-Picture Context

When Things Fall Apart

I consulted with a leader who had recently taken over a department that was in turmoil. Tension was high, and this new leader was at a loss about what do to next. After conducting interviews and getting some history, it became clear to me that the group had lost sight of their goals and were frustrated by the number of changes they were undergoing: new administrative systems, new hires, several people were let go, expanding responsibilities, *plus* a new leader. These folks didn't know where they stood or what all the changes meant—let alone where they were headed. The leader struggled with how to move forward with everyone on board.

After a few coaching sessions to discuss the feedback, the new leader realized that his group needed him to be what I called "The Tour Guide" and provide them with a big-picture context for what they were experiencing. He decided to hold a re-orientation meeting to clarify all they had been through, calibrate how things were going now, and reset their goals and objectives for the future.

Creating The Map

The leader began the meeting by drawing a "map," which was actually a timeline of the important phases of development and changes that the group had been through over the last several years. When his team saw the historical timeline marked with significant milestones, they were surprised and encouraged by how much they had accomplished despite all the changes, growth, and downsizing. They also were invited to add other events they remembered so that the entire group could learn the whole story—the big-picture.

By creating a visual timeline, newer team members gained important historical perspective that they could not have learned except by putting together bits and pieces of stories they heard. Having the big-picture provided by the timeline discussion helped these new employees get up to speed more quickly. It also connected the dots in a meaningful way for the employees who had been there for awhile.

After reviewing where they were and how they got there, the team and their leader talked about what they wanted and needed to accomplish in the future. They explored the realities of where they were right now and identified what they would continue doing, stop doing, change, or create in order to achieve their goals. At the end of their discussion, each team member had a clear understanding of where they were headed and what was expected of them.

Getting Everyone Back on Board

In this situation, the leader acted as "The Tour Guide" to make sure the people on his "tour" understood the new itinerary and how it had changed. By putting everything in context, the group could reorganize and reorient itself. The leader couldn't accomplish this by struggling to get everyone back on the tour when only *he* knew where it was going.

You also don't need a team in meltdown to use The Tour Guide Technique. Leaders I have coached use the timeline map to talk about the history of their group and what they have accomplished so that everyone gets on the same page about the ground they have covered and the problems they have solved. Then, with a sense of confidence and clarity, the team can check their current alignment with the overall company and department goals. These teams value knowing what everyone else is working on and how the entire big-picture fits together. They even notice overlaps, redundancies, and gaps, and then work to fix them.

COACHING RECOMMENDATIONS

What if leaders were more like tour guides? Let's look at what actual tour guides do to create a cohesive experience. Tour guides take charge of the itinerary, point out the highlights, and provide narration of the entire journey. They remind you of where you have been, tell you where you are now in relationship to the destination, and point out major changes that affect timing and direction. They help you value and appreciate the journey. They connect all the dots of the different tour stops by providing you with overviews and details. They also communicate frequently—and if you get lost, you know exactly where to find them.

This isn't to imply that, like the tour guide, a leader already knows everything about the journey. Sometimes leaders are more like explorers headed for a new world—they navigate the unknown, steering by the stars, weather, and ocean currents. Leaders who are "explorers" working in unmapped territory can still communicate the basics to let the crew know they how far they have come, how well they are doing, and how far they have to go until they expect to arrive at the intended destination.

Keeping your team informed about the big-picture becomes more complex when your team is distributed globally. Leaders who integrate elements of the tour guide approach, and include *all* members of their global teams, find that those they lead become more empowered to make decisions and take actions that align with the direction in which everyone is headed—no matter where each team member is located on the map.

HOW YOU KNOW WHEN YOUR
Team Needs a "Tour Guide"

- You usually won't know unless you ask them. Often teams are too busy to stop what they are doing and request a big-picture re-orientation. It doesn't mean they wouldn't benefit from being reminded of where they are and how they are doing.
- You are surprised by what you hear in meetings that indicate people in your group may be duplicating work or are unclear about their roles, goals and responsibilities.

QUESTIONS TO ASK YOURSELF

- How can my team or organization benefit from periodically reviewing where they are in relation to the strategic goals?
- Even if I *think* I do provide opportunities for my organization to regroup and realign with the strategic direction, would those I lead agree? When was the last time I checked?

YOUR CHALLENGE

1. Rate yourself on your current use of **Real Power #7: Provide the Big-Picture Context**

    _____ I need to develop
    _____ I do fairly well
    _____ I'm totally skilled

2. At your next staff meeting, ask your team if they would find value in periodically reviewing what they have accomplished and where they are in relation to the department and strategic

goals. Make it sound like an informative, interesting concept, not just another meeting to attend. Ask them to help design the meeting or process by which you could all accomplish this big-picture review. Or hire a consultant to conduct the first meeting and help you develop a template for future meetings.

3. How can you apply **Real Power #7** to increase your own leadership effectiveness?

CHAPTER 12

SPOTLIGHT MOMENTS—USE 'EM OR LOSE 'EM

Leadership is an action, not a position.
—Donald H. McGannon

Your leadership territory includes what I call "Spotlight Moments." Often leaders are uncomfortable being in the spotlight. As a result, they prefer working behind-the-scenes and dodging the visibility of Spotlight Moments as often as they can.

Wise use of your own Spotlight Moments means knowing when, where, and how to show up with formal messages that inform, realign, encourage, and inspire, both within and outside of your organization. Spotlight Moments need to be planned and carefully interwoven into your leadership agenda and schedule. Your visibility in those moments is really about maximizing your service to your team. To be effective, leaders must be seen and heard.

Real Power #8 :
Maximize Your Spotlight Moments

Mark's Story

Mark was a senior director of a high-tech company. When I asked how he created visibility as a leader, Mark replied that he hired talented, capable people who were strong leaders. He allowed them to do what they did best—take charge of their own areas of the business. He figured they didn't need to hear him stand up at team meetings and give rah-rah speeches. That wasn't his style or what his team expected of him. They all knew what he was thinking, because he held regular one-on-one meetings with his direct reports. As far as being visible outside of his own organization, Mark felt his main focus was within his own area. Besides, he had no time in his busy schedule for additional activities that he felt didn't directly support his team.

During one of our coaching sessions, I asked him if he thought his team might need something more from him. He said he would be surprised if they did, but agreed to a quick survey of his direct reports.

The feedback I gathered for Mark was clear. Here is what his team had to say: "We need to hear from Mark. We'd like to get some formal messages on where we are and what things look like up ahead. He needs to address the entire group and tell us the 'state of the union' and his perspective on things. When he talks to us in a group meeting, we'll know that we all are hearing the same message."

They also added that Mark needed to "show up more at other leaders' meetings to build bridges and get some positive messages out about the work our team is doing to benefit the company overall." Several people said it would help them, as well as enhance Mark's leadership perception, if he traveled to meet with the sales teams and other segments of their organization that were located in various parts of the world. They also mentioned a number of meetings and events within corporate that he could attend to boost visibility and credibility of their entire team.

As we explored the feedback Mark received from his team, he realized that they wanted him to step into the spotlight to do what only he could do for them in his role as leader. He was depriving his team of the visibility *they* needed to be successful—they needed him to increase his visibility both inside and outside the organization. They wanted him to use his leadership spotlight to align their team, shape perceptions, and spread messages that were important for the group as a whole.

Mark, who saw stepping into the spotlight as self-serving and something that made him personally uncomfortable, was surprised to learn that his team had described his leadership role in much broader terms than he did. He would need to expand his vision of his leadership territory from one-on-one conversations to more group and high-visibility activities. He also realized that he would need to improve his skill level in speaking to groups and inspiring confidence in order to maximize his moments in the spotlight.

Identifying Spotlight Moments

In our coaching sessions, Mark noted on an annual calendar what internal group meetings he needed to schedule. He also identified when he needed to travel to different global sites where his team was also located. Then he began to identify other meetings and events where it made sense for him to show up.

Mark could see that if he scheduled his "visibility" regularly and had an extremely clear agenda for what he needed to accomplish, he could shift from avoidance and reactivity to actually being eager to use the spotlight to energize, clarify, and connect with his team and others outside his team.

Mark created a plan, and he began to work his plan with a heightened sense of its importance to the success of his organization. In the process, Mark also discovered that he was an excellent speaker when he was clear on his mission—in this case, it wasn't to promote himself but to respond to what his team requested of him.

COACHING RECOMMENDATIONS

Here are some suggestions for maximizing your own Spotlight Moments:

- Remember that Spotlight Moments come with your leadership territory, identify your key opportunities, and *plan* to use them wisely.
- Step back and see how widespread and deep your actual leadership territory is. You'll find, as Mark did, that it often extends far beyond your immediate team. Claim all of it, and design how you can use it to best serve your team and their goals.
- Use travel and internal meetings to accomplish what can only be done by you, in person. Ask what your team needs to hear from you, and make that your agenda. Your role is to inform and inspire.
- Use your Spotlight Moments to show up as the leader you aspire to be.

HOW YOU KNOW WHEN YOU ARE
Missing Spotlight Moments

- You like working in the background and sticking to business. If people see you out in the organization, you believe they'll wonder why you aren't doing your job.
- You currently don't have anything on your calendar that you would consider a Spotlight Moment.
- Not many other departments or groups in your organization know what value your team provides or what they have accomplished. Worse yet, not many people outside of your team even know who *you* are.

QUESTIONS TO ASK YOURSELF

- How many times have I stepped into the spotlight in the last six months? Were there times I could have but chose not to? Could my lack of visibility be hurting my team?
- Where, when, and with whom do I need to become more visible as a leader?
- Have I asked my team what more they need from me? Have I asked them how I can best represent them throughout the organization?
- How do I show up as a leader when the spotlight is on me? What does the feedback tell me? Is that how I want to be perceived? Could I use some training to boost my confidence and comfort level in speaking?

YOUR CHALLENGE

1. Rate yourself on your current use of *Real* **Power #8:**
   Maximize Your Spotlight Moments

   ____ I need to develop
   ____ I do fairly well
   ____ I'm totally skilled

2. Identify one way you can become more visible as a leader. Ask your team what they need from you, and set up a team meeting to provide that information. Or you can identify an opportunity outside of your immediate team. Make the necessary arrangements. Prepare and step into the spotlight. Afterward, evaluate how it went. Ask for feedback. Make adjustments in your content and delivery style. Look for your next Spotlight Moment.

3. How can you apply *Real* **Power #8** to increase your own leadership effectiveness?

CHAPTER 13

LISTENING AND PATIENCE: STRENGTH OR WEAKNESS?

The key to everything is patience. You get the chicken by hatching the egg, not by smashing it.
—Arnold H. Glasgow

To develop a team that is competent and confident, you need to step back from being in the center of all the action and start using skills that many action-oriented leaders find very challenging: listening and patience.

Often viewed as passive skills, leaders can miss the powerful impact of *listening* to what their teams need and exercising *patience* in letting their teams work through the learning experiences required to be successful.

Real Power #9 : Develop Your Team Using Listening and Patience

Carl's Story: The Firefighter Approach

As vice president of worldwide customer service, Carl even referred to himself as a "firefighter," because to him, all customer problems were like burning buildings. The problem was, he had taken on the task of being the first to run into each building and put out the fire.

Carl's rationale for his approach was: "I've done this so many times, I know what do to. I don't—and the customer doesn't—have time to put up with us floundering around. When my direct reports come to me, after they've described the situation, I know exactly what needs to be done. I almost can't *wait* for them to finish what they are saying, and most of the time I don't. I take charge and just start telling them what to do. Or, most often, I just go do it myself, with them trailing behind me."

Carl's strategy worked until his company and his span of control grew—more customers meant more burning buildings. He was stretched to the max and didn't see how he could handle it all. Then he grew impatient with his team. Why weren't *they* handling these things?

Carl had hit the pivotal point in leadership where he had to set up a new game plan or go up in flames himself. His health and family life were suffering, and he was getting frustrated and impatient with his team.

First he tried the "abandonment method," where he just abruptly stopped handling things and told the team to go it on their own. He watched over their efforts, and then jumped in to undo those efforts if he didn't like the direction they were headed. He still wouldn't let go.

I started working with Carl when he reached a deadlock: he knew he needed to change or perish . . . but how?

Crafting a New Approach

When I talked to his team members, they were crystal clear: "Carl needs to step aside and let us do our jobs. If we come to him for advice, then we expect him to give it. Until then, he can focus on the work he needs to do: getting us resources, talking with high-profile customers, and making sure that the company pays attention to the voice of the customer."

In our coaching sessions, we began to craft Carl's new role. Where would he focus his efforts if he weren't on the ground fighting those fires? His team had told him exactly what they needed from him, so we began to design a plan that put him into a more strategic role. Not an easy task for a hands-on leader.

Carl began by redefining his relationship with his team. He had tried a total and sudden hands-off approach, and that hadn't been successful. For him to step aside and let them do their jobs, Carl needed to build his team's strength and confidence, as well as his confidence in them.

Carl also learned from his previous attempt that he must inform his team that he was changing his leadership strategy. It would be important for his team to understand the changes, what would be expected of them, and the new roles they would all be taking on. He also wanted to know what they would require from him to be successful.

Instead of continuing to identify with his exciting firefighter image, Carl created a new one. He would think of himself as the coach or *guide on the side,* allowing his team to be the ones in action on the playing field. He was amused by the image of a coach grabbing the ball, as he was now doing, and running it down the field to score the winning goal.

Growing a Team through Patience and Listening

Patience and *listening* are behaviors that did not fit in Carl's model of hands-on problem solving. Those qualities did, however, fit the model of a leader preparing his *team* to excel.

Carl knew his leaders would need to feel comfortable coming to him for advice without his taking over the project. As a coach, he needed to back off and have the *patience to listen* and to support his team.

When he redefined his mission from *taking over* to *growing his team,* patience came more naturally. He needed to listen to his team members, not to solve their problems, but to understand how *they* were solving it. Carl learned that patience is not passive. Patience and support from him would help his team develop the skills and have the experiences they needed to meet the demands of their expanding customer base.

Carl also learned that changing his leadership contract with his team was a *process.* It was not as if he could just flip a switch and things would be different.

Within six months, Carl had made significant progress. More of his schedule was focused on strategic issues, and his team members were getting more comfortable taking charge of their own areas. Carl and his team were also working the transition together. Carl could remind them of his expectation that they solve their own problems, and his team could point out when he stepped over the boundary and started doing their work or where he needed to be more involved. Carl felt he had a much better leadership strategy in place to meet the challenges of their organization's future growth.

COACHING RECOMMENDATIONS

Trying to be patient when every muscle in your body is twitching to go into action is next to impossible. And listening becomes a struggle when you believe you know all the answers. This is why leaders find it so difficult to have the *patience to listen*. You need to think differently to truly build a new framework for your leadership.

Having the *patience to listen* can give you much insight into the following:

- How your team members think and problem solve
- The relevant facts in any situation
- The skills and knowledge levels of the players on your team (have you got a bench of A, B, or C skill-level players?)
- What you need to provide, and what they've got handled

Something else to consider: What model of leadership are you using as a basis for *not* using *patience* and *listening* as important leadership qualities?

The bottom line: If you are doing it for them, they aren't learning. If you must be hands-on, be a hands-on teacher, with your goal being to see that your team has the thinking processes and skills to tackle the problems. It requires a shift in how you see yourself as a leader. Do you want to leverage and grow your people's capabilities, or attempt to be in control and everywhere at once? You get to choose your philosophy and your fate.

HOW YOU KNOW WHEN YOU ARE
a Firefighter

You may be a firefighter-style leader if you do the following:

- Put in long hours and are directly involved in every aspect of your department or group's work
- Find that your employees look to you for all the answers and seem unwilling to take the initiative
- Have moments when you wonder why it's all up to you, but you rationalize that that's what you are getting paid to do
- Feel overwhelmed but see no other options for doing things differently

QUESTIONS TO ASK YOURSELF

- If I am proud of being a firefighting, hands-on leader, how is that *really* working for me? Is there another way of leading that would better serve my team and me?
- How many hours am I putting in at work each week because I am convinced that nothing will go right if I am not in the middle of the action?
- How much is my team learning? And how do I know?
- Remember that classic question: "What would happen if you got hit by a truck?" Ask yourself this: "If I weren't around, would my organization be able to carry on without me? Would they be prepared, experienced, and ready?"
- How can I begin to value *having the patience to listen* and see it as an important way to build my team's capabilities and confidence?

YOUR CHALLENGE

1. Rate yourself on your current use of *Real* **Power #9:**
   Develop Your Team Using Listening and Patience

   > _____ I need to develop
   > _____ I do fairly well
   > _____ I'm totally skilled

2. Identify one aspect of your leadership for which you would like
   your team to start taking more responsibility. Meet with them as
   a group, tell them what you'd like to do, and ask how they see
   that happening. Lead a conversation to address the following:
   What would they need from you in the way of support?
   What decision-making authority would they need? How would
   they be accountable?

   Agree to check in with them, as a team and individually, in
   a week to discuss progress and problems. Make necessary
   adjustments and continue checking in until they are through the
   transition period and they are handling that area on their
   own. Then select another area to delegate. Notice how you use
   listening and patience to build the skills and confidence level of
   your team.

3. How can you apply *Real* **Power #9** to increase your own leadership effectiveness?

CHAPTER 14

WHERE ARE YOU LOOKING?

You've got to think about "big things" while you're doing small things, so that all the small things go in the right direction.
—Alvin Toffler

If you want to continue advancing in your career, you will need to demonstrate an ability to pay attention to the details, the short term, the mid-term, the big-picture, the future—the local and the global—regardless of which perspective comes most naturally to you.

The real key is taking the time to consider multiple perspectives and *communicating* what you see.

Real Power #10 :
Communicate a 3-Level Perspective: Ground Level-Hilltop-Helicopter

Joe's Story

Joe, a director of a technical area in a midsize company, got feedback in his leadership assessment that indicated he was "not strategic." Joe didn't agree, saying he knew what was going on around the company but always put his primary emphasis on the work his group was producing.

When I gathered more in-depth information for him from others in the organization, he was further described as "a short-term thinker," "intently focused on the day-to-day," and "swamped in the details." His direct reports were concerned that his heads-down approach wasn't providing them with the broader perspectives they needed. They wanted to know that Joe was tuned in to the rest of the organization. Joe's colleagues saw him as focused solely on the work of his own group and oblivious to work being done in their areas. His boss and other executive leaders saw him as having depth in his technical area, but not the strategic perspective that would make him a good leader in the long run.

Joe felt that all this additional feedback was wrong. He thought of himself as a strategic thinker and leader. Before he ignored an important message from his direct reports, colleagues, and senior staff, I invited him to explore a little further.

Strategic Self-Check

As a first step in taking a closer look at the feedback he received, I suggested that Joe ask himself this question: How do I *demonstrate* that I do, in fact, have a strategic focus?

Joe answered the question by saying that he did his formal strategic thinking once a year during a goal-setting process he was required to do. As far as communicating it to his direct reports was concerned, he felt that they incorporated the bigger picture into the annual department goals, so there was no need to talk about it further. He also realized that he never mentioned strategic issues with his colleagues or boss because meeting times with them were short and he needed to focus on the critical day-to-day business that required their immediate attention.

Joe began to see that about 2 percent of his time was focused on things beyond his group's everyday operations. Doing the self-check opened Joe up to considering that the feedback he received might be more accurate than he would like to admit.

Getting a 3-Level Perspective

Joe realized that he needed a way to expand the amount of time he focused on strategic issues. He still wasn't sure how to "talk" strategically or gain acknowledgment for being a strategic thinker. I assured him that there was a way and it was easy to do.

We worked together to set up a new thinking structure that included expanding his perspective to three levels: close-up, medium range, and long range. We jokingly agreed that he needed to get some "altitude" to avoid focusing exclusively on the day-to-day details. Using a 3-Level Perspective, Joe could ask himself the following questions:

- What's happening at **Ground Level**? This perspective would concern the close-up details of what was going on in his department in the short term. He already did this well.
- What did things look like from the **Hilltop**? This mid-range perspective would get him out of the details and looking at an overview of his team and other departments interfacing with his team. He could also look out weeks and months ahead to anticipate potential threats and opportunities.
- What did things look like from a **Helicopter**? This long-range perspective would include what was happening with

his group, the company, their industry, economic indicators, and stakeholders. From this altitude, he could also consider a more global perspective.

Joe thought that having the additional images of standing on a hilltop and looking around from a helicopter would help him to remember how considering only one level of detail inhibited his vision as a leader. If he wanted to be a strategic thinker, he would benefit from having the perspectives from multiple levels.

Don't Just Stand There, Say Something

Joe also needed a way to communicate his 3-Level Perspective so that others could receive the benefit. We set up the following conversational lead-ins he could use:

> **Level 1 – *Ground Level Perspective***: "At this point in time, this is what we are doing in our department . . ."
> **Level 2 – *Hilltop Perspective***: "However, when I step back and look out three to six months and consider what could potentially happen, I see . . ."
> **Level 3 – *Helicopter Perspective***: "Then, looking out even further and considering the future needs and global trends we are seeing…"

Joe realized that these conversational frames gave him a way to communicate that he was indeed a strategic leader who was tuned-in to and talking about tactical *and* bigger-picture perspectives. He had the mind-set and tools he needed and was ready to give them a try.

Practice + Reflection = Change

We then set up a coaching "practice field" that allowed him to make some commitments and test them out. Joe decided he would do the following:

- Devote one hour per week to strategic think time, during which he would consider all three perspectives: Ground Level, Hilltop, and Helicopter. Joe requested that I work with him during these meetings. He knew that he needed some support in shifting his focus up to the Hilltop and Helicopter levels until they became more integrated into his thinking.
- Schedule meetings with one colleague each week to discuss his or her strategic perspectives.
- Set up one session per month of his weekly one-on-one meetings with his boss to share his Hilltop and Helicopter perspectives and ask for his boss's perspective.
- Hold a quarterly meeting with his entire team to discuss all three perspectives.

And the Winner Is?

After six months of making his 3-Level Perspective one of his top priorities, Joe wanted to know if he had altered his colleagues' perception of him as a "short-term thinker." The six-month feedback interviews revealed that those who worked closest with Joe were seeing a change. They described it as "a broadening of what he paid attention to and what he talked about." His boss and colleagues reported that he was showing much more interest and attention to the bigger picture. Joe was even invited to join a planning team focused on strategic issues of importance to their organization.

And What Did Joe Report?

Joe felt encouraged by the feedback and had this to say: "I actually *am* a strategic thinker who had no time to get up on the hilltop or into that helicopter. Making the time to consider things from those multiple vantage points made a big difference. It also helped me see that I needed to get out of the details, for the good of my department. I could see better short-term actions to take by look-ing at the longer-term implications. I can honestly say I came up with more creative ways to approach a situation when I paused, stepped back, and got some altitude."

Joe also reported: "My whole leadership team has incorporated the Ground Level, Hilltop, and Helicopter views into our thinking and communication. We are less reactive as a team, and that alone has lowered the stress levels around here. To keep the commitment going, I set up a strategic one-on-one meeting with each of them, once per quarter, to discuss their own 3-Level Perspectives of what they see for their teams."

Feedback Is Food for Thought

Joe also learned some important lessons about feedback:

- If the same feedback is coming from several directions, pay attention.
- What appears to be negative feedback can simply be a signal for your next level of development.
- Do a reality check. If it's not on your calendar, you probably aren't doing it.
- There is a way to do things differently, and it isn't always complicated. It just requires your unswerving commitment to apply it every day.
- A leader who fails to make some changes after receiving feedback similar to what Joe received might find his or her career path becoming limited to one for a detail-oriented, short-term thinker.

COACHING RECOMMENDATIONS

What you pay attention to will be abundantly clear to other people. The questions you ask and the topics of your conversations will all point to where you are looking and what you are thinking about. The leadership territory includes the details *and* the bigger picture, the tactical *and* the strategic. Be sure that you are tuned-in to a 3-Level Perspective and that you dedicate time to discussing what you see from each perspective with your team, your colleagues, and those to whom you report.

If you don't have a natural curiosity about the big-picture, or you consider it unnecessary to getting the work done, like Joe, you can learn. Visualizing the three levels—Ground Level, Hilltop, and Helicopter—gave Joe a useful structure to enhance his ground-level-only point of view. Try it and see if it works for you.

Remember, people you lead usually assume that you have access to information regarding the big-picture because of the meetings you attend and the company you keep. You may think you have nothing specific to communicate to your group, but in fact your role is to be a conduit of information. If you stop the flow, the levels below you have only the company grapevine on which to rely. Communicate what you do know (and can share) with them regularly so that they can connect what they do to the larger organizational direction.

As Joe discovered, your colleagues want to know that their interests are being considered in your short- and long-range focus. Your boss and his or her bosses are looking for leaders who keep the entire company's interests in mind, in addition to those of their own department.

HOW YOU KNOW WHEN YOU
Need a 3-Level Perspective

You may be perceived as having a ground-level-only perspective if you:

- Are comfortable with the details but can't remember the last time you stepped back to look at things from a different perspective.
- Have no strategic think time scheduled on your calendar.
- Find that you only talk about what's happening right now.
- Focus your team meeting agendas solely on current issues and problems.
- Get formal or informal feedback that labels you a non-strategic player.
- Aren't invited to serve on committees and task forces that do strategic planning for the company.

QUESTIONS TO ASK YOURSELF

- With which level of perspective do I feel most comfortable: Ground Level? Hilltop? Helicopter?
- Do I have my own way of gaining a balanced perspective between what's happening now, the mid-term, and the long-term?
- What if I used the structure of Ground Level–Hilltop–Helicopter and then communicated what I saw from those perspectives? How would that inform and advance the action in my organization? How would that build confidence in me as a leader?

YOUR CHALLENGE

1. Rate yourself on your current use of **Real Power #10: Communicate a 3-Level Perspective: Ground Level–Hilltop–Helicopter**

    _____ I need to develop
    _____ I do fairly well
    _____ I'm totally skilled

2. At your next staff meeting, use the 3-Level Perspective to communicate how things are going. Practice the conversational lead-ins as you present the information. You might also want to try using the conversational lead-ins in a few informal conversations to test how they work for you. Notice how expanding your perspective and what you talk about affects how you think and contribute as a leader.

3. How can you apply **Real Power #10** to increase your own leadership effectiveness?

CHAPTER 15

THE ONSTAGE/OFFSTAGE DYNAMIC

A leader leads by example, whether he intends to or not.
—Unknown

Not to make you paranoid, but when you are a leader, everyone *is* watching and everything *does* count.

Often, leaders get a little too comfortable and assume what I call an *offstage* persona. They speak or act in ways they wouldn't if they stopped to think about the impact. They simply consider themselves off-camera and off-the-record. The reality is that they are still sending messages, though not always ones that support their true leadership agenda.

It's worth repeating: Leaders are *onstage* even when they are *offstage*—everyone is watching and *everything* counts.

Real Power #11 :
Act As If You Are *Always* Onstage

Onstage/Offstage Leadership Stories

Jerry's Story

Jerry, a senior VP of a research company, walked into work each morning deep in thought. When he passed employees on the way to his office, he rarely acknowledged them. Even if they said "Hello," he didn't respond. In addition, he walked past the same row of cubicles every day, since they were closest to his office. As the day progressed, he would meet with his team and be attentive and engaged in his conversations with them.

When I interviewed Jerry's employees for his leadership assessment, they each thought they had done something to offend him but didn't know what. They said that when Jerry walked by them in the morning, they felt invisible. Many of them commented that he showed favoritism to the people in the first row of cubicles, since he walked through that area every day. Jerry was unaware and his team was demoralized. Jerry figured he was "offstage" and that walking to his office in the morning was time to himself.

Ray's Story

Then there was Ray, the VP of sales for a manufacturing company, who was renowned for having excellent relationships with his customers. Yet his direct reports and others in his organization rated him extremely low in rapport, accessibility, and communication. Where he was attentive to his clients, he treated his staff in an impatient and demanding manner, as if he had two personalities: one onstage, for the customers, and another offstage, for the hired help. Ray believed that customer relationships were his top priority, while relationships with internal staff were not.

Janet's Story

Another leader, Janet, the VP of information technology for a high-tech company, thought she could be totally honest with her team. Feeling completely frustrated with upper management and their lack of understanding and appreciation for the work her department performed, she would roll her eyes and sigh when reporting upper-management decisions during her own staff meetings. She would even make comments about her peers and how this person was an "idiot" or that person was "totally ignorant." Her employees would also hear an expletive or two as she punctuated her descriptions with frustration. Did she mean harm? No. She thought she was offstage, almost as if she were with close friends with whom she felt free to vent.

The Rest of the Story

I interviewed the direct reports who experienced Jerry's perceived snub, Ray's "split personality" with customers and his employees, and Janet's venting during her team meetings. In each case, they interpreted the behavior of their leader as communicating some sort of message. And the message wasn't positive. It affected their confidence and rapport with the leader, and it also undermined trust.

So how did these leaders react when I reported to them the impact of these perceived messages? Each leader immediately dismissed the feedback.

- Jerry said that he wasn't upset with anyone, the idea was ridiculous, and he needed to plan his day while he walked to his office.
- Ray defended himself by saying that he could treat people any way he wanted to if it meant the customer got what he promised them.

- Janet thought her team knew she was just blowing off steam, that they accepted her venting and would keep it all in confidence.

Actually, in Janet's case, the team was upset enough to complain to senior management. They claimed that her venting affected their ability to work with the other leaders she bashed. Her team also wondered why she complained to them about how other managers did not understand the value their team contributed to the organization. Wasn't it part of her job to make that clear? They also wondered what she might be saying about each of them behind their backs.

In talking to these leaders about the impact their behavior was having on their teams, I soon realized that each leader had some degree of the *onstage/offstage* mind-set. There were several questions they needed to answer:

- Now that they knew the impact of their *offstage* behavior, did they need to address it?
- If so, how?
- What if they ignored the feedback and continued doing what they were doing?

Jerry's Responses

Jerry thought his employees' feedback was unfair, but he did acknowledge that it wasn't what he wanted them to think or feel. He also wasn't going to give up his morning think time.

I suggested that he simply make eye contact with each person he passed in the hallway, acknowledge them, smile, and say, "Good morning." If they took that as permission to stop him, he could say he was planning for a meeting and would talk to them later that day. Then he would follow up. He also could change the aisle he walked down each day and, once again, acknowledge whoever was around.

If he chose to do more on some days, he could designate the walk to his office as a time to connect with those who were there. He could reinforce their good work and check in with them informally. He would keep the check-ins brief and upbeat.

Jerry couldn't see how eye contact and a simple "Hello" would change the message the employees seemed to be inventing anyway. I assured him that being seen and acknowledged is high on everyone's list, and also that it's often the simplest things that can make the biggest difference. Besides, I wasn't making this up, for his employees told me exactly what he could do to send a different message. Everyday leadership can be that subtle.

Jerry agreed to give it a try. When we talked later that month, he reported that he actually felt better coming into the building with a simple way to build relationships and remove this impression his unconscious behavior was creating.

Checking back in with his team, I found that they noticed and appreciated this change in Jerry's behavior. Now that he acknowledged them in that *offstage* moment of walking to his office, they no longer felt invisible or wondered what he thought of them. Jerry's small gesture sent a positive, genuine, message of respect to each member of his team and reinforced his *onstage* message of how he truly valued each one of them.

Ray's Responses

When Ray and I discussed his feedback, he said, "I get great results for the company. So changing isn't something I think I need to do. The customers get the best of me, and that's the way it is."

This was one of those situations where the organization's culture didn't support learning, change, or anything but the bottom-line results. So Ray did what he did best and ignored the rest—which happened to be the people who worked for him.

Was he a top salesman? Yes. Was he a leader of people? No. Ray missed the opportunity to inspire his team to support him in serving the customer. He was a one-man show. He left the company when a competitor offered him more money.

Janet's Responses

Janet didn't think her attitude showed. When the feedback gave her a clear picture of how she behaved when she considered herself *offstage*, she wasn't happy with what she saw. Nor was she happy with upper management and her colleagues. She was willing to address both issues.

In several coaching sessions, we identified what was making her so disgruntled with her peers and upper management. She listed ways she could begin to address those issues and take more positive action. We set up vent time during our coaching sessions so that she would have an appropriate place to air her frustrations, and we limited that time to five minutes per coaching meeting. After five minutes of venting, I would request that she shift gears and start looking for ways to reframe her thinking about the issues.

Most important, we reviewed and reset her personal vision for her leadership role. Janet had lost touch with what she wanted to create and build as a leader in that company. She needed to get back on course and back in touch with her best leadership intentions and behaviors.

Doing nothing was not an option for Janet. Sorting through the issues that had collapsed into one all encompassing feeling of irritation and overwhelm was the only way she could get back on track. She realized that inspiring her team was her real intention, and venting her frustrations was not the way to do that.

Janet shifted her mind-set, owned her behavior and its unintended impact, and then acted from her revived intentions of leading, motivating, and inspiring her team. Inspired herself, she also started being a stronger advocate for her department. With her peers, she created realistic expectations rather than promising a service level her group wasn't staffed to provide.

Janet was clear that her *offstage* behavior was not working as a way to deal with the bigger challenges that she faced. She recommitted to leading the team in positive ways. And how did her team members respond to the changes? They felt both relieved and excited about the renewed energy and focus of their leader.

COACHING RECOMMENDATIONS

Again, not to make you paranoid, but when you are a leader, everyone *is* watching and everything *does* count. As a leader, you are *onstage* even when you think you are *offstage*. It comes with the territory. Make sure, wherever you are, that you send conscious messages that support your bigger leadership agenda.

You can see the impact that the leaders in these stories had on their employees by simply not acknowledging someone in the hallway or insensitively venting personal frustrations.

Self-awareness and feedback are extremely important in monitoring the subtle yet high-impact aspects of your leadership. Being unaware is no excuse. Know the impact that *all* your behaviors are having, and pay attention to those that may be hurting rather than helping you. Big changes can often be accomplished with awareness and simple shifts in your behavior.

HOW YOU KNOW WHEN YOUR
Offstage Behavior Is "Off"

- Someone may point out something you said or did that had a negative impact. You dismiss it thinking you were *offstage* and *off-the-record*, so it doesn't count.
- Most likely, no one will say anything to you and you *won't* know. This is where asking a trusted colleague for specific feedback may be the only way to find out.

QUESTIONS TO ASK YOURSELF

- Can I think of times I might have slipped into some *offstage* behavior in my own leadership environment?
- How do I react to other leaders who seem to have different *onstage* and *offstage* behaviors? Does it affect my opinion of their credibility?
- Do I have a confidential, professional relationship where I can vent and sort out my thinking so that what I communicate as a leader is clear and ready for prime time?

YOUR CHALLENGE

1. Rate yourself on your current use of **Real Power #11: Act As If You Are *Always* Onstage**

       _____ I need to develop
       _____ I do fairly well
       _____ I'm totally skilled

2. Try this self-observation practice for one week (or one day): Notice if you have an *offstage/onstage* dimension to your leadership mind-set. When do you think you are *onstage*, and when do you think you are *offstage*? How does your behavior change? Notice also when, where, and with whom you vent your frustrations. Could you be unknowingly undermining your credibility in any way? Whom could you ask for feedback?

3. How can you apply ***Real* Power #11** to increase your own leadership effectiveness?

CHAPTER 16

"SAVE FACE" TO KEEP 'EM IN THE RACE

Whoever acts with respect will get respect.
—Rumi

The Japanese have a tradition called "saving face," which means, "to maintain one's dignity." In the Japanese culture, it is important to avoid doing anything that would cause someone to "lose face."

I use this tradition of "saving face" as a teaching metaphor for the leaders I coach who believe they can get better results by being "tough on people." When these leaders focus exclusively on driving for results, they lose sight of an essential part of leading—a relationship of mutual respect with the employees who achieve those results.

Real Power #12 :
Show Respect for People You Lead

Leadership Stories

When I interviewed employees of leaders who were effective, and in many cases revered, these employees reported that they felt respected and valued by their leader. In return, those leaders had gained their employees' loyalty and wholehearted commitment.

Your effectiveness as a leader in maintaining a high-performing team lies in your ability to keep things on track while showing respect for those involved. You can avoid insensitive, unintentional disrespect by being aware of what you do that results in your team feeling valued and respected—and what you do that has an opposite effect.

Can Praise Have a Negative Impact?

At her department meetings, Nancy consistently praised one particular employee. She held him up as a model of excellence, pointing out how his integrity, work ethic, and results always exceeded her expectations. Nancy thought she was challenging and stimulating others to perform their jobs with equal accuracy and integrity.

So what was the real impact of Nancy's praise? The larger part of Nancy's team felt she did not respect the work they did, which was entirely different from the work performed by the singular employee Nancy praised. In reality, the overly praised employee did not enjoy the spotlight or the envious reactions he got from colleagues. Instead of feeling honored, the exalted employee ended up feeling isolated from the rest of the department in which he worked.

Coaching for Nancy

Showing favoritism is demoralizing if others are also working hard to achieve their goals. Unless everyone has tasks and goals that are similar, you may be comparing apples to oranges and showing your preference for apples. In department meetings, focus on what the teams or individuals are doing right, and encourage them to deliver more of that.

If one person is consistently performing above expectations, consider acknowledging him or her in private. Be direct, in private, with any individuals or groups that are underperforming. Your team needs to know that you are clear on who is and who is not performing up to standards and that you are addressing it in a direct and respectful manner with the people concerned.

Nancy and I also discussed how she could use each team's own goals as the standard by which their progress was measured and acknowledged. The teams could then focus on the goals they set for themselves and shift the focus from competing with each other. This would change the game from "pleasing the boss" to "achieving our target goals."

Are We Having Fun Yet?

John was a leader who used teasing and sarcasm to communicate with his team. He would single out an individual and make what he thought were witty comments about any difficulty he or she might be having in achieving his or her target goals. He thought this demonstrated the camaraderie he had with his team members who were all smart, hard working, and top performers in their areas of expertise. He respected them and felt his teasing showed that he wasn't concerned about them solving any problems they faced.

Coaching for John

When I talked to John's team, they pointed out that being teased by their boss in front of their peers was something they did not appreciate. They never knew if there was a message hidden within his sarcasm. They didn't want to show that they couldn't "take it" by asking John if his comments held a deeper message that they might be missing. John's behavior created more confusion than camaraderie. It also led to his team members taking pot shots at each other under the guise of humor.

John was disappointed to learn that his attempts to demonstrate a comfortable rapport with and respect for his team were actually creating uncertainty and uneasiness. He wondered how he could change his approach and still achieve the camaraderie with his team that he desired.

During our coaching session, I asked John to consider the intention behind his comments. Was he using teasing and sarcasm to deliver messages he felt uncomfortable addressing directly and privately with the individual or team? Did his teasing lean toward the negative? Did he make positive comments and then cancel them out with a cutting remark? Could he see how these behaviors might send mixed messages regarding the respect he felt for his team?

John admitted that he could sometimes use humor and sarcasm to communicate messages that were awkward or risky for him, but most of the time, he didn't have a hidden agenda behind his sarcastic remarks. He meant to be funny rather than critical. He could also see how his team could misinterpret his behavior.

John and I worked together to clarify the relationship he wanted to create with his team. He described the qualities of that relationship as: *trust* between him and each person on his team; *freedom* for everyone to speak honestly and openly; and *respect* for his team and the work they do. Using the feedback he had received as his reality check, John knew that teasing, joking, and being sarcastic with his team, met his own needs for inclusion but wouldn't build the relationships he wanted.

John found it was easier than he thought to shift his behavior when he understood the unintentional impact he was having. He decided that being good-natured, open, and giving his team the respect and appreciation they earned was more important than feeling like one of the gang. As John became more authentic, his team relaxed and trusted that he would say what he meant directly and clearly.

Broken Systems

I was called in to work with Linda, a new director of the after-sales department in a successful hi-tech company. Linda explained that she was hired to fix a growing number of errors and performance problems that plagued the department. She found the entire staff to be resistant to making any changes. Top performers were threatening to leave the department if she persisted with her current approach. They claimed that as the company grew, their jobs were becoming almost impossible to do. Linda was trying everything she could to get them to implement her new processes. Making her mark as a competent, new leader depended upon her ability to turn things around.

Coaching for Linda

When I interviewed her employees, they complained that Linda was creating new workflow processes based on her experiences in her previous company without understanding their work and how it might be different. Her new procedures were causing them to make even more errors. She wasn't listening, so they weren't going to cooperate.

As I interviewed Linda, her employees and upper management, it was clear that although no one knew what was causing the error rate to increase, tempers to flare, and the new leader of the group to flounder, Linda was being targeted as the problem. Finding another leader would be a time-consuming process and the group needed help now. The situation had reached a crisis point.

There were definitely issues around Linda's leadership style and approach, but as I delved beyond the people issues and into the systems, the team revealed that the computers and programs they used to gather information and support the customers were patched together and obsolete. Transferring data from one computer system to the two other systems they used was done manually. Errors were frequent since multiple people were responsible for manually transferring large amounts of data and these people were constantly being interrupted by customer calls.

No matter how they scheduled work flow and trained people to do the work, the team would always be behind and making errors as they transferred data between their existing systems. The problems were increasing as the company became more successful and their list of customers grew.

Working Hard and Failing

This team was working hard to overcome the obstacles in the workplace. Getting the critical aspects of their jobs accomplished required a huge amount of effort. From the employees' point of view, they were not appreciated or acknowledged for the work they did and the contribution they made—in spite of the systems. They knew the company expected even more from them than they could possibly provide.

The employees of the after-sales department experienced a lack of respect—no one was listening to them. Instead, they were dismissed and labeled as a group of "complainers" who just wanted to get out of doing their work. In reality, these employees wanted to do such a good job that they actually believed that the problems they faced were because they weren't smart enough to work in the system they were given. Their self-esteem was low and their "voice" in solving the systems issues they faced was silent.

Respect is a System that Works

This story did have a positive resolution. With all the information presented to them, the company acknowledged that the obsolete, incompatible computer systems were the core problem and invested in new computer tracking equipment. The company provided training for the after-sales team and the team worked together to create new work processes. Each member of the after-sales team finally experienced the respect they had all worked so hard to achieve.

Linda continued as director of the department. She had learned that trying to be a superhero and save the day before doing a thorough assessment of the situation didn't work like she thought it would. Leaders often need to focus on getting critical resources before expecting their employees to be top performers. Linda's initial days as the new leader could have been spent exploring the situation and asking questions to identify the real cause of the performance problems.

Respect, as demonstrated in this story, means giving people the tools and resources they need to do their jobs. Respect also means listening and looking deeper into the chronic complaints to discover what's really going on—is it a people, process, resource or systems issue? Or is it some combination of all three? Ultimately, respect means trusting people and believing that they want to do their best and nothing less.

COACHING RECOMMENDATIONS

Showing respect for those you lead is something you may think you already do. If the feedback says your employees feel respected, then whatever you are doing is communicating your respect. If not, you have some exploring to do.

The Gallup Organization has conducted an enormous amount of research through employee surveys that measure employee engagement. The results of this research are reflected in a book, *First, Break All the Rules: What the World's Greatest Managers Do Differently,* by Marcus Buckingham and Curt Coffman, which identifies that employees do not leave companies, but, rather, they leave their managers. Think about it, would you want to continue working for a boss who did not seem to respect you or your work?

Saving face by showing respect doesn't mean you don't deliver hard messages or even let people go. It doesn't mean that underperformers are allowed to continue underperforming "out of respect." Respect is talking to underperformers directly, giving them a pathway for improving and an opportunity to succeed. Their own actions will decide whether or not they course correct and get back on a high performance track. Being clear, direct, and acting with respect can be the best way to keep those top performing "faces" in your organization.

Some Ways to Show Respect

If your goal is to create highly engaged and dedicated employees, then spend some part of each day showing your employees that you respect them. Here are some ways in which you can show respect to your employees:

- Acknowledge them for their contributions on a regular basis. Be sure to spread the praise around and avoid showing favoritism.
- Establish clear performance goals and hold them accountable.
- Give ongoing performance feedback—both positive and corrective.
- Demonstrate thoughtfulness, empathy and kindness.
- Provide them with tools, systems, resources and training they need to be successful.
- Believe in them and listen to what they have to say.

HOW YOU KNOW WHEN YOU AREN'T
Showing Respect

You may not be showing respect for those you lead if you do the following:

- Have a reputation for being intolerant and unforgiving with your employees. You may even take pride in that reputation.
- Find people transferring out of your leadership whenever they can, for reasons you may not always understand.
- You haven't asked your employees for feedback, so you are unaware if they feel respected or not. Lack of respect isn't a topic that employees will bring up on their own. Being respected is a basic need that people have, and is difficult to ask for.

QUESTIONS TO ASK YOURSELF

- Can I remember a time I lost face? How did I feel? How did it affect my confidence and future performance?

- Do I want others to experience those same feelings of diminishment or loss of face under my leadership?
- Would my team describe me as teasing or sarcastic when I communicate with them? If so, do I know the impact that is having?
- Would my team say that I fairly distribute the positive feedback and acknowledgment I give to them?
- Do I make sure my employees have the tools, resources, and systems they need to do their work? Would my employees agree?

YOUR CHALLENGE

1. Rate yourself on your current use of **Real Power #12: Show Respect for People You Lead**

         _____ I need to develop
         _____ I do fairly well
         _____ I'm totally skilled

2. Try this self-observation practice for one week (or one day): Write down three instances when you notice yourself demonstrating respect for your employees. What did you do and what were the circumstances?

   To continue your self-observation notice the following: Do you over-praise certain groups or individuals? Do you use humor and sarcasm to communicate with your team? If you are hearing chronic complaints from employees, have you considered that there may be some process, resource, training or system issues that need to be addressed? How will you investigate further?

3. How can you apply **Real Power #12** to increase your own leadership effectiveness?

CHAPTER 17

DON'T BE THE *JERK* IN A KNEE-JERK REACTION

Speak when you are angry and you will make the best speech you will ever regret.
—Ambrose Bierce

How do you respond if someone you lead takes a risk and fails? Or if someone just plain screws up? Does frustration cause you to lash out at the person or group responsible for the error?

Extending the *benefit of the doubt* to your employees says, "I trust that you were doing your best. Let's find out what went wrong." The problem gets fixed, lessons are learned, and relationships are strengthened. Problems and mistakes are inevitable—you will need trust and strong relationships in place to resolve the next ones that come along.

Real Power #13:
Grant Everyone the *Benefit of the Doubt*

Andrew's Story

Andrew's face was red and his body tense as he stood in the middle of his office, fuming. He launched into a tirade about something a direct report had done, and wanted to postpone our coaching meeting while he went and ripped into this person with his full wrath. Rather than grant his request, I asked if he would be willing to pause and consider some other possible actions he could take. Andrew reluctantly agreed.

Cool Down: From Angry to Curious

I asked Andrew to tell me what happened. He did, letting me know how this was one of the worst actions this person could have taken in this situation. After listening a few minutes, I asked, "What would make this person do something like that?" He said he didn't know. Then I asked, "Are you sure of the facts?" He paused and replied, "Not completely, but from what I do know, he's wrong!"

Then I asked, "How important is your relationship with this direct report?" He said the relationship was an important one, since this person was in charge of a large part of his organization. Then I asked him how jumping into attack mode would solve the problem, especially when he didn't have all the facts or an understanding of why this employee did what he did. Could he potentially be creating a backlash that would damage trust or the ability of this employee to admit and learn from his mistakes?

I also asked him if blowing off steam directly with this employee was the best use of his leadership influence? What was he modeling? Did he realize that his behavior would be replicated throughout his organization as "the way we solve problems and treat people around here"?

I could see Andrew calming down as he considered my questions. He had been caught up in the moment. Pausing allowed him to realize that he didn't have the full story and was about to damage an important relationship.

A New Approach

After cooling off and considering the long-term potential impact of his immediate response, Andrew created a whole new strategy for handling this issue. He opted to stay calm and find out the facts first, as opposed to acting on assumptions; to solve the problem, rather than assigning blame; and to maintain an important relationship, not ruin one, by granting his employee the benefit of the doubt regarding his actions.

Later That Day . . .

In a follow-up phone call the same day, Andrew thanked me for inviting him to pause and reflect before leaping into possibly harmful action. He had talked with his direct report, and with more of the facts on the table and the direct report's explanation of why he had taken the action he did, it turned out to be a mix-up with the client that could be easily fixed.

The problem got resolved and the relationship was strengthened. This wouldn't be the last problem they would need to solve together. Andrew also provided an example to the rest of the team (all of whom were watching everything) for how problems got solved and people got treated in his organization. Had he continued out his office door that day, in confrontation mode, he would have sent quite a different message.

Andrew jokingly asked me if I could stand outside his office door to avert any future disasters. I reminded him that he had all he needed for those future situations. The main thing he needed to do was recognize his angry feelings, then pause and cool down before taking any action—especially ones he might regret. Replacing anger with curiosity would serve him better.

While he paused, he could ask himself the questions I had asked him:

- I know I'm angry, but am I sure of the facts?
- What long-term negative impact could venting my angry feelings have? Is it worth it?
- What would make this person or team do what they did?
- How important is my relationship with this person or group?
- Am I extending the benefit of the doubt to the people involved?
- What leadership behavior do I want to model?

Andrew concluded our check-in call by saying, "I can see where I don't need to be superhuman. I'm entitled to be upset. But now I have another way of handling it. As the leader, I'm also visible, and I want to be proud of what people see. Pausing to cool down and then granting others the benefit of the doubt is more in line with the kind of leader I aspire to be."

These are the breakthrough moments that remind me how much I value my work as a leadership coach. These everyday decisions and actions, when handled with self-awareness and integrity, really do make a big difference. They are pivotal points that either continually build your leadership credibility and align you with your goals or take you off course. Andrew made choices that kept him on course.

COACHING RECOMMENDATIONS

No leader aspires to become the "jerk" in a knee-jerk reaction. If you lash out in anger, you can cause long-term damage to relationships and diminish trust—a high price to pay for mindlessly venting your emotions. Cool off, be curious, and get the facts straight first.

This "cool-off first" strategy also applies to sending angry emails. It's fine to write them to sort out your thinking and vent your feelings—just don't hit the Send key. Hit the Save key instead, read it later and edit accordingly. Or don't send an email at all. After you've calmed down, most problems can best be resolved with an in-person conversation—or phone call if there is distance involved. You want to solve the problem not create reactions you aren't even there to observe. One-sided, flaming emails are famous for causing more collateral damage than positive outcomes.

Don't think granting the benefit of the doubt means that you also have to condone incompetent skills or behaviors. If someone lacks skills or is making poor judgments, granting the benefit of the doubt allows you to gather all the facts first. Given what you discover with an open and curious approach, you will know if the employee needs additional training, coaching, or even to be reassigned.

HOW YOU KNOW WHEN YOU ARE
Venting

You may not be extending the benefit of the doubt if you do the following:

- Get angry when things go wrong and feel justified in venting your anger on whomever you assume to be the guilty party or group.

- Send flaming emails when you are angry. You might even think this provides the individual receiving the email with insight into how their actions have affected you, the company and perhaps the entire world.
- You apologize when you jump to conclusions and vent your anger thinking that shows you are a reasonable and understanding person. (I know a leader who would routinely send flowers to employees on whom she had vented her wrath.) It doesn't convince anyone, but you wouldn't know that without specific feedback on the actual impact your angry outbursts have on your team or organization.

QUESTIONS TO ASK YOURSELF

- How do I typically behave when I am angry or upset about a problem in my group? How did I handle the last situation that was serious enough for me to get involved?
- How much attention do I give to maintaining relationships when I must get derailed projects back on track?
- Do my direct reports think of me as a leader who grants the benefit of the doubt as a consistent leadership behavior? Do I know that for sure?
- Have I ever hit the Send button after writing an angry email when I should have saved it and edited it later or not sent it at all? How did or didn't that email positively contribute to resolving the problem?

YOUR CHALLENGE

1. Rate yourself on your current use of *Real* **Power #13:** **Grant Everyone the** *Benefit of the Doubt*

   _____ I need to develop
   _____ I do fairly well
   _____ I'm totally skilled

2. Think about an example of when you did extend the benefit of the doubt to someone. What did you do and what were the circumstances? What was the outcome? Do you think it is a practice that creates a better *quality* outcome? If you don't normally extend the benefit of the doubt to others how can you begin?

3. How can you apply *Real* **Power #13** to increase your own leadership effectiveness?

CHAPTER 18

THE *KNOW-IT-ALL TRAP*

It's not hard to find smart people.
It's hard to find people who inspire and motivate.
—David Maister

Can leaders who ask "smart questions" be as effective as leaders who are smart and have all the answers? If the leader always knows the right thing to do, it can create a dependency and lack of independent thinking on his or her team.

Being able to ask intelligent questions—with the right intention—is one of the most powerful leadership skills you can develop.

Real Power #14 :
Lead with Questions

Paul's Story

Paul was a senior director and smart, extremely smart. He had earned advanced degrees from top universities. Early on in his career, he was rewarded for his ability to quickly arrive at solutions to complex problems. However, as he moved up the leadership levels in his organization, Paul was getting feedback that troubled him and his manager. Paul came to his first coaching meeting with one question: "Why do I rate so low on my leadership assessment?"

When I observed Paul meeting with his direct reports, I saw his quick thinking in action. During discussions or problem-solving sessions, he appeared to race to the finish line and present his idea of the right answer while everyone else was still at the starting blocks. Although Paul felt he saved valuable time by "cutting to the chase," there were ideas and considerations that didn't make it into the discussion as others felt cut off and often deferred to his line of thinking.

When I shared my observation with Paul, he explained that: "Yes, I often get to the solution before everyone else—and I am usually right. So how is that the problem? Isn't that what I get paid to do—come up with the right answers and get things done?"

I asked Paul if he was willing to look at how his eagerness to be the smartest person in the room might have gotten him to the head of the class in school, but may not be where he needs to be as a leader?

Here are the points we explored:

- Given that he was leader of an expansive global department, did he have access to all the information he needed to make decisions? Was there a chance that he needed more input before he arrived so quickly at his conclusions?

- Nothing deflates teamwork more than a leader with all the answers. Unless your team members can contribute and their contribution is valued, they will soon disengage.
- Leadership is about facilitating information flow, and about leveraging the intelligence and experience of your direct reports. You will still make the tough decisions, but you'll just get there via a more inclusive and collaborative process.

So what could Paul do differently? He could make his *team* smart by asking questions.

Could Asking Questions Be the Best Answer?

Questions are irresistible to the human brain. Asking questions triggers the brain to engage and stimulates it to think at a broader, more creative level to solve a problem. If Paul used questions effectively, he could stimulate more of the thinking he wanted to encourage on his team.

I explained that asking the right *kinds* of questions is critical. If he just asked questions to lead people to the conclusions he had already made, they would feel manipulated. He needed to ask questions he wanted them to be asking themselves—questions that would reveal their thinking process and what they were considering (or missing) as they worked through issues and made decisions.

In developing his questioning strategy, Paul asked himself the following:

- What's my intention? Will I be asking questions from genuine curiosity or to lead people to what I want them to think?
- What questions will allow me to check my team's thinking process without getting bogged down in the details?

- Can I ask questions that are supportive and empowering instead of questions that undermine the team's confidence?
- Can my questions contribute to building the caliber of thinking we all use to share information, solve problems, and make decisions?

Paul was intrigued. He knew he possessed great analytical skills but thought some of his direct reports could sharpen their own problem-solving skills. He created a few questions he could use to provide a framework for the thinking processes he wanted to encourage within his team. Here is a sample:

- What problem are we solving? Do we all agree on that?
- Who needs to be involved in this process?
- What resources do we need and how will we get them?
- What other groups will be affected by what we do?
- How does this effort support our target goals?
- Is this the right time to implement what we are proposing?

Paul started testing his questions in staff meetings. He began to see that this new approach caused his team to think about any gaps in their process before they went into action. It was clear that starting where his team was and helping them along with questions got the members much more involved in the process. He still could add his ideas, but more subtly, by asking: "What if we thought about it *this* way?"

Paul would not withhold his own opinions in team meetings. He would merely be stating them less often. His direct reports wanted and needed to know his thinking on issues, as much as he needed to know theirs. However, Paul could also slow down the speed at which he shared his thoughts. Others needed to get their own thinking organized so they were ready to listen to what he had to suggest.

We also talked about the way he asked his questions. Paul needed to ask with an open curiosity, plus a willingness to listen to and consider the response. Otherwise, he would not create a safe place for people to take risks. He said he was working on that. His expectation that they should already know what he knew had a tendency to make him impatient.

The CEO with One Powerful Question

I shared a story with Paul that illustrates the power of questions.

I observed an executive team meeting in which a human resources director proposed that certain actions be taken to stop employees from using the company e-mail for personal reasons, most specifically posting personal items for sale. There was also an incident where an employee was sharing some damaging gossip and hit the "worldwide distribution" option, and everyone in the entire company around the globe got the e-mail. There were clearly some issues around using the company e-mail appropriately and strictly for business that needed to be addressed.

The HR proposal was highly punitive. The announcement that the HR director read was to be sent out to all employees. It set down the new rule that the company e-mail could no longer be used for personal use. Anyone caught doing so would be disciplined.

The notice went on to describe the impact of accidentally sending out global e-mails. It threatened that no more incidents would be tolerated, and any employee sending e-mails for worldwide distribution without authorization would be strongly reprimanded.

The HR director paused after reading the announcement. He wanted the executive team's approval before it was published to the company. He received only silence. It seemed like a proper way to chastise the guilty, if that was what they wanted to do.

The CEO asked one question: "How does that announcement support our values?" You could almost feel the breeze as the direction of thinking shifted in the room. This company had just spent months revitalizing its company values, which included creativity, teamwork, and respect. Everyone in the company had participated in the values clarification process. They had stated, loud and clear, that what made this company special was the people who worked there.

The HR director thought about it a moment and replied: "It doesn't. Let me take this and rework it."

The HR director returned the following week with an announcement that included the following:

- To accommodate the needs of people within the company who wanted to offer their items for sale, a new online bulletin board would be established for employees. A team would be set up to create any guidelines for the bulletin board that would help the site operate effectively.
- A request was made that since there would be a place for all classified ads, the company e-mail would be used for company business only. If there were other employee groups that needed to be formed, HR would be interested in hearing any and all suggestions.
- Reference was made to the e-mail that accidentally went worldwide. This time, employees were reminded of that impact and asked to think twice before they sent any e-mail. HR made some simple guidelines for e-mail etiquette available online.

The executive team approved the revisions and agreed that this approach did, in fact, support the company values. The employees were delighted with the announcement. They now had a legitimate place for communicating and posting items for sale. They viewed it as the company being responsive to their needs. In return, they felt more than willing to keep the company e-mail reserved for company business. They also appreciated the information and guidelines on Internet etiquette. Since they all had received the e-mail that went worldwide, they knew the impact it could have. Lesson learned.

Paul was impressed with the power of that single question. He could see a number of ways that scenario could have gone, and none of them would have created the spirit of cooperation required to truly resolve the issues.

Paul also saw how the CEO was keeping his eye on the big-picture—in this case, the company values. The CEO needed to see how this action lined up with those bigger values to which the company was committed. And he needed to act in a way that was creative, showed respect, and supported teamwork. He had accomplished all of that with his one powerful question.

Now Paul was beginning to see that he didn't always need to jump in and beat everyone to the finish line. Paul didn't stop being smart—he just started being smart in a different way.

The Follow-Up

Six months later, we did a follow-up assessment with Paul's team and found that his scores on leadership were moving up. His team commented that they felt they had more room to share their thinking. They liked questions that challenged them. And they did not like questions that made them feel stupid or criticized them in front of their colleagues. Gradually, they were building their own processes to answer the questions they knew Paul would be asking. They were also starting to use the same questioning approach with their own direct reports.

Paul continued to refine both his questions and the way he asked them. He was enjoying the challenge, the improved quality of thinking he was observing, and the fact that it was changing perceptions of him as a leader in the eyes of his team.

COACHING RECOMMENDATIONS

Often leaders benefit from a redefinition of what it means to be "smart, "intelligent," and "effective influencers." Talking, telling, or being the smartest person in the room may be personally satisfying, but as a leadership behavior it may not be serving you as well as you might think.

Using questions effectively requires paying attention to how you want to operate as a leader. There are times when you can make more of a contribution by stepping back and asking questions that focus on the process and thinking involved, versus jumping in and showcasing your own ability to think quickly. When you do share the results of your quick thinking, tell people how you got to that conclusion. Revealing how you connected the dots to come up with your answers can also serve as a thinking model for others on your team.

Although *what* questions you ask are critical, *how* you ask them is just as important. The intention behind your questions will determine the quality of your responses. Questions meant to push your way of thinking by "leading the witness" are only covers for a not-so-hidden agenda.

The intention behind smart questions is to stimulate thinking, create a safe place for ideas to be considered, and enable you to guide the process. Focusing on the *process* of how things are getting done and what your team is *thinking* can make you a much smarter leader in the long run.

HOW YOU KNOW WHEN YOU ARE
Being *Too* Smart

- You are most comfortable when you are telling and talking. You don't much care what others are thinking, as long as they know what *you* think.
- It feels good to get to an answer quickly and share it with others.
- You often hear yourself deflecting suggestions by saying, "I already do that."
- You can't remember any good questions you have asked lately. If you do ask a question, it is to challenge a fact or statement someone else has made.
- You rarely ask questions about the process being used or the thinking being applied.
- You were impressed with the story in this section about the CEO who asked one question that created an entirely new solution. You realized it would never occur to you to do something like that.

QUESTIONS TO ASK YOURSELF

- How can asking smart questions be more powerful than having all the answers?
- How can I use questions to get the best thinking activated in individuals and teams that I lead? What are some good questions I could use?
- How can I ensure that the intention of my questions is perceived as sincere and not manipulative? How can I keep from sending a message to my team that I will let them talk but I will reveal the *right* answer when they are done?

YOUR CHALLENGE

1. Rate yourself on your current use of *Real* **Power #14:**
   Lead with Questions

   _____ I need to develop
   _____ I do fairly well
   _____ I'm totally skilled

2. Come up with some "million-dollar questions" you can use to stimulate and check the thinking taking place within your team. Like the CEO who asked his million-dollar question: "How does this proposed action support our values?", you can identify powerful questions that work in most situations. Then start asking your questions at your next staff meeting and notice what happens. Inform your team about what you are doing so that they understand your shift from *telling* to *asking*. Give them time to adjust to your new approach.

3. How can you apply *Real* **Power #14** to increase your own leadership effectiveness?

CHAPTER 19

WHAT ELEPHANT?

Smooth seas do not make skillful sailors.
—African proverb

It's revealing to ask leaders about their metaphor for conflict. When I ask them to finish this sentence, "Conflict is _____," I usually get answers like: "my worst nightmare."

In business, conflict comes with the territory. There are too many differing perspectives and objectives to assume that conflict sparked by those differences will not be a part of getting things done. Avoiding honest, open discussion of differences results in the creation of the "elephant" that everyone sees but won't mention for fear that things will get out of control.

As the leader, how *you* define and handle conflict has a lot to do with how conflict is handled in your team or organization.

Real Power #15:
Proactively Manage Conflict

Pat's Story: A Positive Example

Pat, a senior leader I interviewed while writing a research report on women's leadership, has one of the best mind-sets regarding conflict that I have encountered. She recognizes that conflict is inevitable whenever you have creative people working together. Her top priority is, "Creating the best organization we can while building strong relationships as we go. We want to deliver the best service possible, create an organization we all want to be a part of and attract customers who want to work with us."

Pat believes that without valuing relationships, respect for each other would be lost, and constantly repairing respect takes too long given that the next conflict, or "set of differences," as she calls them, is just around the corner.

Pat gives her teams this directive for dealing with conflict, "We can disagree, but at the end of the day, I want you to ask yourselves: How can we get to the other side of this disagreement with the best decision made and our relationships intact? How do we get the best of our thinking out in the open and a decision that we all agree to support even if it requires that we 'agree to disagree'? All those involved need to be heard, respected, and included in order to understand the logic of why a certain approach would be chosen over another."

This leader has set the "rules of the ring," and no one was going to get knocked out in the process. If Pat saw that conflict was brewing, she quickly got the people together to work things out before the conflict grew. She would often facilitate conversations, or provide a neutral facilitator, so people could work through their differences. She encouraged respectful language and thoughtful consideration of each point of view.

Pat's ground rules helped her team to work through most conflicts on their own. Competition was considered healthy, creative differences were expected and their process was constructive. Her organization even created a motto to remind them of the way they wanted to deal with conflict: "May the best idea win, but we won't defeat each other in the process."

COACHING RECOMMENDATIONS

Interpersonal conflict is a primary cause of breakdowns in work and information flow. As a leader, it is essential that you provide the ground rules and context for how to work through conflict within your team. Being personally uncomfortable with conflict is not a valid reason to avoid it.

What if you, like Pat, reframed your view of conflict from something to suppress to a "sometimes uncomfortable process required for creativity and innovation"? What if people remained in conversation about differences instead of becoming entrenched in their own positions and fighting to win?

If conflict is a fact of organizational life, what if your job is to develop structures and processes that productively orchestrate conflict? As a leader, not accepting conflict as part of the territory keeps you from creating an environment or culture that acknowledges conflict as normal, and has ways of working through it.

Too many leaders escape dealing with conflict by telling their employees: "You work it out among yourselves" and walk away convinced that this is a strong leadership move. It is not. I have been in meetings when the two employees on opposite sides of a conflict are attempting to work it out. With no existing ground rules in place, it requires that one or both have the maturity and skills to step out of the heat of the disagreement and think logically and fairly. It's a rare person who can do that. They also may not have all the information they need to make a balanced decision.

Even professional boxers step into a ring governed by rules they know and a referee to call the game when rules get broken or the action gets out of hand. The boxers' objective is to win. That's what they are trained to do. Your managers and direct reports are also trained to win. That's how they got to where they are.

Unless you always want the ideas of the strongest, cleverest "fighter" to prevail, you need to provide a safe "ring" for people with differing ideas to work things out. Your job is to level the playing field so that all ideas are heard and considered, and all creative differences are examined for merit and used to serve the bigger objectives that need to be met. As challenging as it may seem, addressing conflict is a skill that can be learned.

Guidelines for Proactively Managing Conflict

1. You first

If you have a weak muscle when it comes to handling conflict, now is the time to build it. Read books on dealing with conflict, hire an expert to coach you, and get some training. Become a "student" of turning conflict into a productive tool for building relationships and promoting creativity. Then you'll have some walk behind your talk when you begin to change the way conflict works in your organization.

2. Create a climate for constructive conversations

As Pat demonstrated earlier in this chapter, articulate and model your philosophy of dealing with conflict for your team. By clearly communicating your directives around how differences are explored, you set the level of integrity and the expectations for how your team handles conflict. Your conflict guidelines should reflect that people need trust, safety, and emotional control in order to talk honestly and openly.

3. Develop team conflict competencies

Those you lead will also need to redefine conflict as constructive and learn ways to communicate more effectively. I highly recommend hiring a consultant who specializes in structures and processes for dealing with conflict to guide your team in developing the necessary skills, behaviors, and agreements they need to be successful.

4. Keep it alive

I've seen leaders and teams work brilliantly through steps 1–3 and then slip back into old conflict averse or destructive behaviors because they neglected to continue building their skill level and holding themselves accountable. That's where you come in. Leaders continue to keep important issues alive when the novelty wears off. Repetition of important goals is a large part of any leader's job. Remember, also, that when new members join your team, they need to be brought up to speed with an overview, training, and support on how the team handles conflict in your organization.

HOW YOU KNOW WHEN YOU ARE
Avoiding Conflict

- To maintain the illusion of harmony, there are a lot of unspoken rules in your organization about what is acceptable to say where, when, how, and to whom. In other words, there is at least one elephant in the room at all times.

- Everyone values being nice over being willing to openly and respectfully disagree.
- When a conflict issue is brought to your attention, you hear yourself saying, "I expect you to work it out amongst yourselves."
- There are no actively applied ground rules for dealing with conflict in your team or organization.

QUESTIONS TO ASK YOURSELF

- What is my own comfort level with conflict? Do I view conflict as a constructive process?
- How do I handle conflict as a leader? Are there issues that are just too hot to address, so they become "unspeakable" but ever present, like the proverbial elephant in the room?
- Do I set the guidelines for how to deal with conflict within my team? Is respect and maintaining ongoing relationships part of our conflict-resolution process?
- How can I get training or coaching if I would like to reduce my own discomfort in addressing conflict and setting ground rules for managing conflict within my team?
- How do I model dealing with conflicts I have with my employees, peers, and boss?

YOUR CHALLENGE

1. Rate yourself on your current use of *Real* **Power #15: Proactively Manage Conflict**

     _____ I need to develop
     _____ I do fairly well
     _____ I'm totally skilled

2. Locate reading or training resources that will help you learn some constructive ways to think about and handle conflict. Review the resources to identify guidelines to use for yourself and your team. You can also hire a consultant to help your team address a hot issue and use that experience as a model for handling future conflicts.

3. How can you apply **Real Power #15** to increase your own leadership effectiveness?

PART II SUMMARY

What Do These Leaders Have in Common?

In addition to the 15 *Real* Powers of Leadership presented in Part II, there are some underlying patterns that unite all of these leaders and their stories. Here are some highlights of what these leaders have in common, and what you can learn from them.

Check Your Unintentional Impact

Most of these leaders were so well intended that from their perspectives they were doing everything right. And that was part of the problem. They were *only* considering their own perspectives—and not the perspectives of their employees, colleagues, bosses, and other important players. As a result, they were leading without any real knowledge of how they were being perceived as a leader—and they were unaware of the actual impact they were having.

Feedback Is a Gift—Listen-Up

Did you notice how most leaders were surprised by the feedback they received? Their first impulse was to reject it. The feedback was deemed unbelievable, inaccurate, or unclear, since it pointed to a perception or impact the leader never intended to create. Feedback is one thing most of us are uncomfortable receiving since it has been used more often as a weapon than a tool. When interpreted correctly, what appears to be negative feedback can be an important signal for your next level of development. Before you dismiss surprising feedback, check it out.

Change Begins with You

In most of the stories, you can see that the successful resolution to the problem involved each leader examining his or her beliefs and actions. The leaders soon learned that if *they* changed, they would see changes in others. These leaders found they actually gained an incredible amount of power and control with this strategy.

They were not only in complete control of the things they could change about themselves but they demonstrated that leaders could be flexible and responsive. They added two new questions to their thinking process: "What part did I play in creating this problem?" and "What can I think, do, or say differently to help resolve it?"

Effective Leaders Balance *Results* and *Relationships*

When leaders let their critical relationships slip out of focus, they experienced problems in getting results. Maintaining the balance between getting *results* and building *relationships* is an underlying theme of each leader's story. Unattended relationship issues can derail any project and decrease your influence. Balancing your attention on both keeps everything running more smoothly.

Get Support

Each leader had support (a coach) to help him or her decipher, clarify and accept the feedback they received and then identify specifically what they needed to change. This is very difficult to do on your own. There is an expectation that leaders should already know everything—that's another myth to unmask. Real leaders get support to keep learning and that takes real courage.

The Paradox of Leadership

You also might have noticed through the leaders' stories and the coaching they received, that effective leadership is a paradox. Leaders are expected to:

- Be focused and determined yet consider the perspective of others.
- Be confident and openly seek feedback.
- Drive for results and be sensitive to relationships.
- Change others by being willing to change themselves.
- Be competent and strong at the same time they are open to learning and getting support.

You may be experiencing the tug of these contradictions. The truth is, there is no "one right way" to be a leader. It's not an either/or proposition. Nor do you want to be on "automatic pilot" as a leader. Leadership is a dynamic process that requires balancing the pull between what often appears to be totally opposite ways of being.

Developing self-awareness (what am I doing and how's that working?) and good judgment (what's the best way to lead in this particular situation?) are critical components of effective leadership. It requires being self aware, tuned-in and responsive to the situation and people in front of you.

Do you recall how earlier in this book the research conducted by Jim Collins for his book, *Good to Great: Why Some Companies Make the Leap . . . and Others Don't*, was cited as discovering Level 5 Leadership—the highest level in a hierarchy of executive capabilities? Collins described the Level 5 Leader as "a study in duality: modest and willful, shy and fearless." He was describing the paradox of leadership we have been exploring. It's interesting that what appears at first to be a perplexing paradox is actually the "duality" demonstrated at the highest level of leadership.

You may also recall that Collins found the leader with the larger-than-life persona was *not* the person at the helm of companies that were moving from good to great. Leaders don't have to be superheroes if companies are destined for greatness. Now that's a paradox!

> *How wonderful that we have met with a paradox.*
> *Now we have some hope of making progress.*
> —Niels Bohr

Questions to Ask Yourself

- What other observations do I have about the leaders' stories in Part II?
- What insights did I gain from their stories and coaching?
- What can I apply to my own leadership situation?

Part III

Put It All Together

Leadership is much more an art, a belief, a condition of the heart, than a set of things to do. The visible signs of artful leadership are expressed, ultimately, in its practice.
—Max DePree

Since **Leaders Don't Have to Be Superheroes** is meant to be a call to action, there are several levels of action you might consider at this point.

Level 1: Sharpen Your Awareness

The stories and coaching points have triggered your awareness and you may now begin noticing what you haven't noticed before in your own leadership practices. You may also become more aware of the impact your own Leadership Force Field is having on others. You can use the tools in Part III to continue sharpening your awareness.

Level 2: Test Out a *Real* Power of Leadership

You resonated with several of the stories and coaching recommendations in Part II and you are interested in trying out at least one of the 15 *Real* Powers of Leadership in your own leadership territory. Part III will provide you with support and the tools to begin. There is a summary table of the *Real* Powers of Leadership that you can use to identify which of the powers you want to develop further.

Level 3: Change Your Game

You may be at a pivotal point in your leadership. You may have gotten your own wake-up call through feedback you have received. Or you may be looking for a way to take your leadership to the next level. For you, this book is the spark that ignites your own quest to increase the value you bring to your leadership role. The tools in Part III will assist you in getting started. Game on!

CHAPTER 20

SELF-ASSESSMENT:
THE *REAL* POWERS OF LEADERSHIP

One must learn by doing the thing;
for though you think you know it,
you have no certainty, until you try.
—Sophocles

The *Real* Powers of Leadership presented in Part II are summarized in the Self-Assessment Table on the next several pages. As you review each *Real* Power in the table, do a quick self-assessment or refer back to how you rated yourself at the end of each chapter in Part II. Decide if you are already skilled at using that *Real* Power or if it is one you would benefit from developing.

Once you've identified the *Real* Powers you want to develop, you'll be guided through some steps to get you started.

Self-Assessment:
The *Real* Powers of Leadership

In which of the *Real* Powers of Leadership are you skilled, and which could you develop further? Check the appropriate box on the right-hand side of the table. Before checking the "Skilled" column, make sure you can think of several examples of when you have effectively demonstrated using that specific *Real* Power.

The *Real* Powers of Leadership Self-Assessment

Real Powers	Develop	Skilled
#1: Create a Safe, Collaborative Environment Is *The Blame Game* being played in my organization? At what cost?		
#2: Align Your Expectations, Words, and Actions Do I unintentionally send mixed messages to my team because my expectations, words and actions are not aligned? How would I know?		
#3: Model What You Expect of Others Does feedback tell me that I model what I expect of my employees?		
#4: Build a Relationship Network How balanced is my *Relationship Bank Account*? Am I building a network of support beyond my own team?		

Real Powers	Develop	Skilled
#5: Optimize Your Daily, Informal Communications In my everyday conversations, what messages am I sending through my words, tone, and body language?		
#6: Maintain Rapport with the People You Lead How am I building rapport with the people I lead? Am I allowing technology to replace personal connection?		
#7: Provide the Big-Picture Context How could acting as *tour guide* help my team stay connected to the bigger context of our work?		
#8: Maximize Your Spotlight Moments How am I using the visibility of my *spotlight moments* to maximize my service to my team?		
#9: Develop Your Team Using Listening and Patience Do I currently consider *listening* and *patience* to be valuable leadership skills? Am I actively using them to develop my team?		
#10: Communicate a 3-Level Perspective: Ground Level–Hilltop–Helicopter Am I usually focused on the details or the big-picture? Do I consider a *3-Level Perspective* and communicate what I see?		

Real **Powers**	Develop	Skilled
#11: Act As If You Are *Always* Onstage Is my behavior when I am *offstage* consistent with my *onstage* behavior? As a leader, when do I think I am ever *offstage*?		
#12: Show Respect for People You Lead In what ways do I *save face* and demonstrate respect for those I have the privilege of leading?		
#13: Grant Everyone the *Benefit of the Doubt* Do I extend the *benefit of the doubt* to everyone instead of jumping to conclusions about people and situations—especially when things go wrong?		
#14: Lead with Questions Am I willing to give up being the smartest person in the room and make my team smart through the *questions* I ask?		
#15: Proactively Manage Conflict How do *I* handle conflict? Have I set up expectations and guidelines for how conflict can be a constructive process in my team or organization?		

Review the *Real* Powers Table and notice how many you checked as "Skilled." Congratulations, you are already leveraging these powers to increase your credibility and influence as a leader. Continue to apply them and build your skills in those areas.

Which *Real* Powers Will You Develop?

Notice how many of the *Real* Powers of Leadership you checked: "Develop." Which of those would you like to put some focus on developing? Which could have the biggest impact in your particular situation?

On the lines below write the top three *Real* Powers of Leadership you would like to develop over the next three months. You may, however, have more than three or only one or two that you have identified. Plan to focus on one *Real* Power each month.

1. *Real* Power #: _____: _____

2. *Real* Power #: _____: _____

3. *Real* Power #: _____: _____

Select the *Real* Power you will work on during the first month:

> *Real* Power #: _____:
>
> _____

The upcoming chapters will support you in building your Development Game Plan.

CHAPTER 21

A FEW WORDS ABOUT LEADERS AND LEARNING

Leadership and learning are indispensable to each other.
—President John F. Kennedy

When it comes to learning, leaders often get tangled up in a lot of *shoulds*: "I *should* already know how to do that, I *should* be able to learn that on my own, and it *shouldn't* take so long for me to see results." Sounds like our superhero expectations surfacing again.

Some leaders think that they don't have to learn anything new to be effective. They just do what they think they *should* do or what leaders they've had in the past have done. Unfortunately, that's like saying you can conduct an orchestra if you've watched someone else do it and you are able to hold a baton and wave your arms gracefully—it's obviously more complex than it looks.

And as for using other leaders in your organization as role models—organizations are notorious for promoting people who push for results without paying attention to building relationships, gaining trust, influencing, communicating, collaborating, inspiring, and setting an example. All of the relational qualities required for building a sustainable, global business culture that will attract and retain the top-tier employees a company needs to be successful.

Unless you have role models who demonstrate leadership characteristics that move companies forward in today's global economy, you may be perpetuating leadership behaviors that serve no one.

The bottom line is that the nature of leadership is changing and there is much to learn. It's important to see leadership and learning as "indispensable to each other." Dropping the expectation that you *should* already know everything about leadership is a big step in the right direction.

Learning to Learn

Learning to improve your leadership is no different than learning anything else—similar rules apply. Think about something you do really well. There was probably a time when you weren't as good at it, but you wanted to be. You most likely started somewhere on the learning curve and worked your way through some frustrating attempts and less-than-stellar performances. There were probably many times you thought that you *should* be doing better than you were. Yet, you persevered until you achieved the level of proficiency you sought.

You may have even hired someone with the expertise or skill you needed to train and guide you. You knew you could fast track your learning with some one-on-one support. Learning is a *process* that requires *practice with feedback*. And you don't need to do it on your own. You can use mentors, executive coaches, and training programs to keep you accountable and challenged.

Learning also takes *patience* and *time*. Do you think that you don't have the time to learn anything new? Remember the story of "Daddy" Don in Chapter 6? No matter how long Don continued to avoid his team, they weren't going to become the independent, creative go-getters he wanted them to be unless he stopped doing what he was doing and tried something different. He was stuck and his team was stuck. Imagine how much time that uses up. The futility of repeating behaviors that aren't getting you the results or the responses you want is often more time-consuming than learning to do things differently.

Another essential aspect of learning is *inspiration*. Clarify your incentive for learning. It could be achieving a new level of expertise, creating a legacy or having a smoother running organization—a team that operates with less "noise" and fewer breakdowns in getting things done. Figure out *why* you are learning a new leadership skill, and that will keep you inspired.

Making a commitment to your own learning will keep your leadership on the cutting edge. You will be sharp and operating in the moment—drawing from your wealth of experience but not being restricted by it.

Remember, even the best want to get better and you never want to stop learning—*especially* when you are a leader.

CHAPTER 22

CREATE YOUR DEVELOPMENT GAME PLAN

Even if you are on the right track,
you'll get run over if you just sit there.
—Will Rogers

Here are some suggestions that can assist you in creating a learning strategy for the *Real* Powers of Leadership you choose to develop.

Getting Started

Creating a Development Game Plan will prevent other priorities from pulling your focus away from your learning commitment. Set up your plan like a game: define what you want to achieve, create a timeline, and identify benchmarks to measure your progress. If you want a coach to work with you on this process, now is the time to get one involved. You may have internal coaches available or prefer to hire an outside coach.

Define What Success Will Look Like

Before you begin, define what it will look and feel like when you are successfully using the *Real* Power of Leadership you want to develop. High achievers often don't envision a finish line and if they do, they keep moving it—always believing they can do better and depriving themselves of a sense of accomplishment. You can keep developing your skills—just define success for this phase. Be realistic about what you can accomplish in a month or six months, or whatever you have set up as your timeline.

Find Your Inspiration: Why Are You Doing This?

Without inspiration, you will probably lose interest in your goal after the first day. Take some time to answer these questions: Why do I want to develop this *Real* Power of Leadership? What will it do for me? How does it fit into the bigger picture of who I want to be as a leader? What is the prize I'll want to keep my eye on when the going gets a little rough? What thought would keep me on track when events conspire to challenge my commitment?

Form a Support Team

Identify the players you want on your team—trusted colleagues, bosses, and employees who can provide support and feedback. Most people won't volunteer to give you feedback unless you request it. You can also give them permission to give you feedback whenever they observe something they think you may be unaware of and could benefit from knowing.

At a minimum, ask a trusted colleague to give you real-time feedback after a meeting or event where you have practiced a new approach. Leaders who do this gain tremendous respect. Rarely is requesting feedback perceived as a weakness. It is most often viewed as you taking charge of building your strengths as a leader.

Identify Your Starting Benchmark

You have a much better chance of making appropriate changes when you know where you are *now*.

Benchmark #1: Self-Observation

Start off by observing yourself in action around the *Real* Power of Leadership that you want to develop. For example, if you are working on *Real Power #4: Build a Relationship Network*, keep the idea of building relationships in the front of your mind for the first week. What do you notice? Are you building relationships in ways you had not recognized before? Or do you notice that connecting and building relationships is not on your mind at all?

What impact do you think you are having as you move through your day? Take notes. Awareness is the first step.

Benchmark #2: Request Feedback

Now is the time to call on your support team. Decide who can give you the most useful feedback to calibrate what you are doing well and where you need to change in the area you are developing. You can also work with your coach to help you design an efficient, effective way to gather feedback that will point to exactly what you should be working on.

Set Up *Practice Fields*

When you have targeted specific behaviors you want to try out, identify *where* you would like to practice these new behaviors. The event or conversation you identify is then called your "practice field." You are setting up a framework that helps you to focus on one particular leadership skill in a specific scenario where you can practice and do some trial-and-error testing. Working with your practice field goes like this: you will set your intentions for using the new skill or behavior, participate in the conversation or activity, note what happens, and evaluate how you did. Following your evaluation, you will know what worked and what didn't. You then can identify other practice fields for additional practice and testing until you feel comfortable using the new skill or behavior.

Continue to Get Feedback

You can't be sure that you are making progress until you do a reality check. You might find that you are doing even better than you think you are! If you find that you *aren't* doing as well as you expected, then you will have gathered some specific information to work with. Set up other practice fields, observe the results, and then check with others to see if your observations are accurate. This is a key component of the learning process: test and validate.

Practice Pausing

As you practice new leadership behaviors, remember that the need for speed when you are learning is not a priority. Slow down. Pause. Take a deep breath, and *choose* your responses, rather than continue to *react* in habitual ways. Pausing suspends action so that you can insert a new behavior, a new way of thinking, another way of saying something, or any other new learning you want to integrate into your leadership style. Otherwise, the old pattern or behavior is set in motion without a second thought, and you'll miss some golden opportunities to implement your intended new way of doing things.

Pausing is powerful because it leads to informed, inspired action—and that's the best kind.

Get a Coach

To be honest, this is a difficult process to manage on top of all your other responsibilities. If you opted out of selecting a coach in your original Development Game Plan, and you are having difficulty with maintaining focus and accountability, now may be the time to change your mind. You can work with a coach for whatever length of time you choose, to help you with the following:

- Interviewing others to collect information on your leadership impact
- Observing you in action and giving you unbiased feedback
- Clarifying the feedback so that you know what to do differently
- Supporting and guiding you in making any necessary changes
- Providing customized, private training sessions to help you build a skill area
- Suggesting relevant outside training or conferences, as appropriate
- Creating a regular check-in schedule and keeping you accountable
- Helping you measure and acknowledge your progress
- Keeping you inspired

After One Month, Check Your Progress

Check your progress at the end of your first month and see how you are doing. Compare your results against how you defined "success" before you started. Acknowledge your progress—perhaps even celebrate it. High achievers often rush past the opportunity to reward and acknowledge their own efforts and achievements on their way to the next goal. Take time to mark your wins and thank your support team.

Evaluate Your Development Game Plan

Next, you'll want to evaluate your Development Game Plan and make any changes that will make the plan work better in the future.

Select the Second *Real* Power You Want to Develop

Are you ready to take on the second *Real* Power you identified for your development? If so, create your new Development Game Plan, and begin. When you've developed your second *Real* Power, you can then move on to the third, and so on.

Pause, Reflect, and Review

At the end of three months, you will have practiced the top three *Real* Powers of Leadership you targeted for development. Reflection and review is a critical part of learning, so stop and ask yourself:

- How am I doing?
- What's different as a result of my efforts?
- Does the feedback from others match my own observations?
- What's my ROI (return on investment)?
- How will I continue to practice these *Real* Powers of Leadership?

Keep in mind that long-term results and the ease with which you execute your newly acquired *Real* Powers of Leadership will take time to show up. Be patient and persistent, as you would when learning anything new.

CHAPTER 23

LEADERSHIP IS WHAT YOU DO EVERY DAY

Nothing so conclusively proves a man's ability to lead others as what he does from day to day to lead himself.
—Thomas J. Watson, Sr.

While you are working on developing your specific *Real* Powers of Leadership, you are still a leader each and every day. Therefore, it might be helpful to ask yourself a question that will serve as a daily warm-up for the important role you play in your organization.

A Powerful Question to Ask Yourself Every Day:

What is the single most important *leadership* activity I want to accomplish today?

Your response to this question becomes your leadership goal for the day. Setting your daily intention around leadership keeps you aware and focused on stepping up and claiming your leadership role— every day and in every way.

Setting Your Daily Intentions

If you make a habit of considering your leadership intentions each day, then it follows that you can start writing them down, just as you would your list of tasks to accomplish. In our task driven work environments, keeping your leadership commitments visible and distinct reminds you of that critical role that you accept every day when you show up for work.

One Final Story: Nate's *Revised* Daily Priority List

I recently worked with Nate, a senior director in a hi-tech company, who kept a small piece of paper in his shirt pocket. He showed it to me several times over the course of the year that I was his coach, when he wanted me to see his top priorities for the day. Of course, he had his electronic planner that documented his very busy calendar—and his assistant kept him completely organized and on time. But on the piece of paper he carried in his pocket, he wrote the things that meant the most to him to achieve that day.

When we first started working together, the items on his list were urgent tasks he needed to complete. All of them were short-term, tactical actions. One year later, Nate showed me his daily priority list so that I could see how he had revised it.

Nate's *Revised* Daily Priority List

Action Items:	Leadership:
• Complete budget report	• Inspire my team today
Strategic Actions:	• Ask questions: Be Patient & Listen
• Plan goals for India trip	

Nate reported that, once he had expanded his list to include strategic actions and the quality of his *leadership*, along with the tactical actions he needed to take, he found himself behaving differently. He was more conscious of the actual impact he was having as a leader, as well as the impact he *wanted* to have. He thought about the relationships he was building and took concrete steps to communicate more of what he knew people needed to hear from him.

By adding the second column to his daily priority list, Nate had done something quite subtle, and yet it represented a *major* shift in his thinking and ultimately in who he was as a leader—every day.

CHAPTER 24

SOME FINAL THOUGHTS

Throughout this book, you've read the stories of leaders who had the courage to become the best leaders they could be. Their stories demonstrate that leaders are human, not superheroes—and that it takes a lot of character and determination on a daily basis to grow into your full potential as a leader.

At the heart of each story is the undeniable fact that leadership begins with YOU: *who* you are, *what* you do, *how* you do it, and the *impact* you have on others. Your leadership is inseparable from who you are as a person and your interactions with people. Your beliefs, values, thoughts, and talents all influence how you lead.

As I said in the beginning of the book, you are invited to learn from each leader's story and the coaching they received. May you be inspired to explore the leader you are and the impact you have on those you lead—and then make changes for the better. What your organization and the world need now is good people being good leaders. Let it begin with you.

Watch your thoughts, for they become words.
Watch your words, for they become actions.
Watch your actions, for they become habits.
Watch your habits, for they become character.
Watch your character, for it becomes your destiny.
                                        —Unknown

Appendix A

REVIEW QUESTIONS

1. What is your current model of leadership? Is it time to update it? When was the last time you changed anything about the way you lead and who you are as a leader?

2. Have you debunked your own myth about leaders having to be superheroes?

3. Do you believe you can *learn* to be a better leader?

4. Have you accepted the idea that being a leader is about who you are in the interactions you have every day?

5. Do you see that your leadership role is a distinct set of knowledge, skills, and behaviors that you need to be constantly aware of applying and improving?

6. Can you see that leadership is subtle and powerful at the same time?

7. Are you ready to be aware of and care about your impact on others?

8. Do you see how a dual focus on task *and* relationship is the best way to get work done in an organization?

9. Would you say that your Leadership Force Field inspires others and creates an environment in which people can do, and want to do, their best work?

10. Can you see how feedback is a gift? What system do you have in place for consistently collecting feedback?

11. Have you defined your personal metrics for success as a leader? How can the *Real* Powers of Leadership be the basis for your own personal leadership metrics?

12. Do you realize that in order to be inspiring, you must first be inspired yourself? What inspires you about your leadership role?

Appendix B

The 15 *Real* Powers of Leadership Index

BIBLIOGRAPHY & SUGGESTED READING

Baldoni, John. *Great Communication Secrets of Great Leaders.* New York: McGraw-Hill, 2003.

Bennis, Warren and Burt Nanus. *Leaders: The Strategies for Taking Charge.* New York: Harper & Row, 1985.

Blanchard, Ken, and Michael O'Connor. *Managing By Values.* San Francisco, Berrett-Koehler, 1997.

Bridges, William. *Managing Transitions: Making the Most of Change.* Addison-Wesley, 1991.

Buckingham, Marcus, and Curt Coffman. *First, Break All the Rules: What the World's Greatest Managers Do Differently.* New York: Simon & Shuster, 1999.

Collins, Jim. *Good to Great: Why Some Companies Make the Leap . . . and Others Don't.* New York: Harper Collins, 2001.

Covey, Stephen R. *Principle-Centered Leadership.* New York: Summit Books, 1990.

Dotlich, David L., Peter C. Cairo, and Stephen H. Rhinesmith. *Head, Heart & Guts: How the World's Best Companies Develop Complete Leaders.* San Francisco: Jossey-Bass, 2006.

Fisher, Roger and William Ury. *Getting To Yes: Negotiating Agreement Without Giving In.* New York: Penguin Books, 1983.

Goleman, Daniel. *Emotional Intelligence: Why It Can Matter More Than IQ.* New York: Bantam Books, 1997.

Hesselbein, Frances. *Hesselbein on Leadership.* San Francisco: Jossey-Bass, 2002.

Kouzes, James M., and Barry Z. Posner. *The Leadership Challenge.* San Francisco: Jossey-Bass, 2002.

Martin, Andre. *The Changing Nature of Leadership*. Research white paper from the Center for Creative Leadership, CCL© 2007.

Naisbitt, John. *Megatrends: Ten New Directions Transforming Our Lives*. New York: Grand Central, 1984.

Patterson, Kerry, Joseph Grenny, Ron McMillan, and Al Switzler. *Crucial Confrontations: Tools for Resolving Broken Promises, Violated Expectations and Bad Behavior*. New York: McGraw-Hill, 2005.

President and Fellows of Harvard College. *Harvard Business Review on Leadership*. Boston: Harvard Business Review Paperback, 1998.

Ray, Michael and Rochelle Myers. *Creativity in Business: Based on the Famed Stanford Course that has Revolutionized the Art of Success*. New York: Broadway Books, 1989.

Senge, Peter M., et al. *The Fifth Discipline Fieldbook: Strategies and Tools for Building a Learning Organization*. New York: Doubleday, 1994.

Stone, Douglas, Bruce Patton, and Sheila Heen. *Difficult Conversations: How to Discuss What Matters Most*. New York: Penguin Books, 2000.

Weiner, Allen N. *So Smart But...*. San Francisco: Jossey-Bass, 2007.

Wheatley, Margaret J. *Finding Our Way: Leadership For an Uncertain Time*. San Francisco, Berrett-Koehler, 2005.

Wycoff, Joyce. *Transformation Thinking*. New York: Berkley Books, 1995.

ABOUT THE AUTHOR

Bonnie Gallup, MA, has been a successful leadership and organizational consultant for over 25 years. She started her own consulting firm, Bonnie Gallup & Associates, in 1981 and her business continues to be generated by referrals from current and former clients.

Bonnie uses a holistic approach in working with leaders—focusing on improving their job performance while emphasizing the human factors that make the difference between being an ordinary and extraordinary leader. She builds enduring relationships and often works with her clients over many years of their careers.

Bonnie has coached leaders at all levels throughout the United States, England, Japan, and Malaysia. A partial list of her client companies includes: Intel, Network Appliance, Xilinx, Apple Computers, Coherent Laser Group, Hewitt Associates, Towers Perrin, General Electric Nuclear, Marriott Hotels, and San Jose State University.

Bonnie has a BS in Education, an MA in Educational Technology and a Master's certificate in Neurolinguistics. She has served on the board of the South Bay Organizational Development Network, Global Women's Leadership Network and the UC Berkeley Human Resources Extension Program. She was an adjunct professor at San Francisco State University and taught courses at UC Berkeley Extension. She has published articles on leadership coaching in *Vision/Action: The Journal of the Bay Area OD Network* and *Consulting Today*.

Raised in a military family, Bonnie has lived in Japan, Turkey and 8 different states in the USA. She has a global perspective that she continues to develop as she travels for work and pleasure. Currently, Bonnie makes her headquarters in Northern California where she enjoys a fulfilling work life. She loves travel, hiking, photography, and writing. She claims the only way to truly experience a culture is by sampling the local cuisine—taking pictures as you go. Bonnie has been married for 31 years to husband, Joe. Their grown daughter, Megan, has circled the globe in her own travels.

You can contact Bonnie on her website: www.bonniegallup.com

WHAT BONNIE'S CLIENTS HAVE TO SAY

Bonnie has the ability to deliver tough, corrective guidance. She is an excellent listener and a powerful motivator. I think her greatest strength is in helping her clients to truly look beyond the obvious, get a sense of what they really want to achieve, and putting together a plan to make that happen. Bonnie coached me for several years and has become the still, small voice of reason in the back of my crowded head.

    —Rusty Walther, Vice President, Technical Services, Hewlett-Packard

Bonnie has done such a wide variety of work in such a broad spectrum of companies that she brings a wealth of experience to every project. She is very creative. It is illuminating to be coached by her. She does not make things complicated, but is direct and to the point in her style, while remaining committed to her coachee's success.

    —Chris Taylor, Vice President of Human Resources, Tabula, Inc.

Bonnie is empathetic to the challenges of leadership but honest regarding what it takes to be a leader. She encourages self-exploration and honesty. She is willing to play "behind the scenes" but is also willing to stand next to me as needed or requested.

    —Julie Murphy, Vice President of Human Resources, Plantronics, Inc.

I was always a skeptic of executive coaches, but Bonnie changed my mind completely. At our first meeting, I told her that "I can't work any harder than 70 to 80 hours a week— why do I seem to be less effective?" She and I focused on that particular problem, but also ended up working on many of my other business/leadership skills. Not only has my business life become better/more effective, but it's spilled over into my personal life as well. I can't even begin to explain what a profound impact Bonnie has had on my career and ability to balance work and life challenges.

   —Nick Howard, Senior Director, Service Operations, Network
     Appliance (NetApp)

Bonnie's way of asking just the right questions, allows me to see new actions to take on old problems.

   —Peg Wynn, Vice President of Human Resources, Atheros
     Communications

About Bonnie Gallup & Associates

www.bonniegallup.com

As the bar keeps rising for innovative products and employee performance, how are you raising the bar on your leadership performance?

At *Bonnie Gallup & Associates*, we believe that extraordinary leadership is a prerequisite for extraordinary business results. Organizations with great products, processes and people need great leadership to truly succeed in the long term.

So how do you raise the bar on leadership in your organization? One powerful way is through *Leadership Coaching*. A leader with a commitment to growth and a dedicated coach can create a customized game plan designed to move his or her leadership effectiveness to the next level with minimal time away from the job. A coach helps a leader to clarify what's important, focus on the right results and stay in action.

Great leaders inspire extraordinary performance in others. An investment in keeping your leaders growing and learning is an investment in your company's bottom line—and its future.

What leaders are saying about Leadership Coaching:

"I can talk to my coach about what's important to me and my work. People outside of work aren't interested and there's no one who can be neutral in my own work environment. There is truth to the saying that it's lonely at the top. Now I can talk through my strategies, put all my thoughts out on the table and work through possible scenarios before I take action. I find that

when my thoughts are clear, my actions can be more efficient and effective. My coach always reminds me of the bigger context, my vision and values whenever I lose sight of them."

—CEO, Hi-Tech Firm

"As my department grows, the need for me to lead and not "do" is absolutely critical. I thought I was doing a great job until my team gave me a very low score on "leadership". My coach helped me clarify, understand and most of all accept the feedback and see why it was important to change. Together we created a game plan. It's a whole new learning curve but I've got great feedback systems built in to track my progress. Working with a coach makes change doable. Otherwise I wouldn't have known where to begin."

—VP of Sales, Semi-Conductor Company

Index

STAYING IN TOUCH

If you'd like more support or ideas for unmasking your own myths and claiming the *Real* Powers of Leadership covered in this book—you can stay in touch through Bonnie's website: **www.bonniegallup.com**

Offers available on the website:

- Free Assessment Tool for the 15 *Real* Powers of Leadership
- Guidelines for leading Team Learning Sessions with your own team
- Additional *Leaders Don't Have to Be Superheroes* Articles
- Executive Coaching

Tell me your stories

Over the years, I have heard leaders say that "we never get to talk to other leaders and find out what they are doing to address some of the challenges we all face." With that in mind, I'd be interested in hearing your leadership stories—problems that had you stumped and how you solved them; how you are applying what you learned in this book; and what's working for you as a leader. If I hear from enough of you, I'll compile and publish on my website your comments (with your permission) and share your collective experiences with all of you.

You can email me at: bonnie@bonniegallup.com

CPSIA information can be obtained at www.ICGtesting.com
Printed in the USA
BVOW040902230911

271870BV00002B/2/P